The European Monetary System:
Its Promise and Prospects

Philip H. Trezise, Editor

The European Monetary System: Its Promise and Prospects

*Papers prepared for a conference
held at the Brookings Institution
in April 1979*

THE BROOKINGS INSTITUTION
Washington, D.C.

Foreword

The European Community, having survived a host of difficulties and crises, as well as extended periods of languor, entered its third decade on a distinctly upbeat note. In June 1979 it took the historic step of electing a European Parliament by popular vote, thus establishing a democratic link between the citizens of the nine present members and the Community's institutions. Less fundamental, but bold enough for a Community still adjusting to its 1972 enlargement, was the decision to take in new members—Greece, Spain, and Portugal—from Europe's Mediterranean rim of less industrialized, lower income nations. A third venture, which is the subject of this volume, is the move toward European monetary integration represented by the creation in March 1979 of the European Monetary System.

At a conference held at the Brookings Institution on April 18 and 19, 1979, the prospects for the new system were set forth in papers by Jacques van Ypersele de Strihou, *chef de cabinet* to the prime minister of Belgium, Michael Emerson of the Commission of the European Communities, Henri Baquiast of the French Ministry of Finance, Robert Triffin of Yale University and the Catholic University of Louvain, and Christopher McMahon of the Bank of England. Their papers, which constitute the main part of the book, are introduced by Philip H. Trezise of Brookings and discussed by four American observers of the system: Ralph C. Bryant and Robert Solomon of Brookings, Benjamin J. Cohen of Tufts University and the Massachusetts Institute of Technology, and William J. Fellner of the American Enterprise Institute for Public Policy Research.

The Institution is grateful to the Ford Foundation and the German Marshall Fund of the United States, whose grants supported the Brookings conference and this publication.

Although several of the conference participants occupy official posts, they wrote and spoke as individuals. Nothing herein should be attributed to the

v

governments and organizations with which they are affiliated. Similarly, the views expressed herein are those of the authors and discussants and are not to be ascribed to the trustees, officers, or other staff members of the Brookings Institution.

BRUCE K. MACLAURY
President

July 1979
Washington, D.C.

Contents

Philip H. Trezise

Political Commitment: The Central Question

Although the subject matter of the European Monetary System is too technical to be front page news, it would be wrong to suppose that it does not have any of the high political significance attached, say, to a European Parliament or Community enlargement. Logically, the process of monetary integration would lead in the course of time to a single European currency, a European central bank, and a European monetary policy—that is, to some of the crucial elements of political union. The proclaimed objectives of the EMS, of course, are considerably more modest: to reduce, not eliminate, exchange rate fluctuations between the member countries and to foster mutually helpful economic policies rather than to require a single policy. Full monetary union, with all its implications for national sovereignty, is not in the present catalog of goals. Even so, the more limited EMS objectives, along with the procedures designed to achieve them, will require much enhanced cooperation among the EMS members. Indeed, the political commitments needed to make the EMS a success are very far-reaching, extending as they do into things usually considered to be rigorously domestic in nature.

At the Brookings conference on the EMS, the question on which opinion divided most sharply was precisely that of political commitment. Are the governments ready to take the hard decisions and carry out the politically charged policies that could give greater stability to exchange rates within the EMS grouping?

Each of the five main essays in this book gives a generally affirmative answer to that central question. All the authors, though writing in different contexts, believe that the EMS will receive the critical measure of official support required to make it work. They do not blink away the problem of the disparate initial rates of inflation among the EMS nations, nor do they assume that the technical features of the new system will operate automatically. But they do consider that the EMS—unlike the earlier, unsuccessful European

1

Monetary Union effort of 1972-73—can overcome the problems ahead because of the flexibility of its design and because of its appeal to the broad political interest of each of the member states.

Flexibility, in the view of the EMS proponents, or optimists, is a key consideration. The aim of a "zone of monetary stability" in Europe is carefully qualified by the recognition that exchange rate adjustments are likely to be needed. Stability is not equated with rigidity. Moreover, the EMS is explicit in its emphasis on the connection between exchange rates and domestic economic policies. Convergence, as Michael Emerson says in his paper, is one of the words most often used in the current discussion of European Community policy. It can mean, for EMS purposes, the narrowing of inflation differentials or, what may be the same thing, the adoption or continuation of stimulative policies in the price-stable economies as the more inflation-prone undergo the necessary decompression. In any case, the EMS begins with an understanding that whether the system stands or falls will depend on the extent to which national policies and performance can be brought into greater harmony.

Convergence is expected to be facilitated by the EMS "divergence indicator." When any EMS currency diverges from all the rest by a preordained percentage, the presumption is that corrective measures will be taken. These could be interventions in the exchange market or even changes in central rates, but it is also envisaged that domestic monetary, fiscal, or incomes policies may be adapted or adopted to cope with the situation. The indicator is to send its signals to countries with strong currencies as well as to those with weak ones; the asymmetry that was a continuing problem in the Bretton Woods system is supposed to be avoided in the EMS.

EMS flexibility, the optimists agree, must be reinforced by political will. Bases for optimism on this count are, first, Europe's disenchantment with flexible exchange rates and, second, the common concern that the European integration process should not be permitted to suffer the serious setback that a breakup of the EMS would represent. Exchange rate fluctuations are believed to have been one of the chief causes of Europe's unsatisfactory employment and growth performance since 1973. The political appeal of an effort to achieve greater monetary stability is founded on the conviction, or hope, that it will help to promote a resumption of the economic expansion so lacking and so sorely missed in the Community. Beyond that, Europe's political leaders will presumably be reluctant to have a major Community project fail. Perceptions of national interest doubtless remain a powerful motivating force in the Community states; but each nation's interest is also seen to include, in some degree at least, progress of the Community toward its integration goals.

Ranged against the optimism of the five EMS proponents was the skepticism, shading into downright disbelief, of the American discussants. Ralph Bryant and Robert Solomon of Brookings, Benjamin J. Cohen of Tufts and MIT, and William Fellner of the American Enterprise Institute were all doubtful that the evident hazards facing the EMS will be matched by an equal measure of political resiliency and fortitude. There was, of course, no challenge to the proposition that convergence of the European economies could establish the requisite conditions for a zone of monetary stability. But with inflation rates varying from 3 to 13 percent in the EMS grouping, the road to convergence would probably be too painful for the shaky economies—and no one could assume that the strong currency countries would or should be willing to inflate up to the rates of their neighbors. It was pointed out that nothing from the recent past argued otherwise.

The American doubters therefore agreed that the EMS objectives ought to be reversed. Coordination or convergence of domestic economic policies should have priority. If this large political order could be delivered, stable exchange rates would normally follow, or at any rate be more easily achieved. Ralph Bryant argued further that, without full monetary union or its near equivalent, an agnostic view should be taken of EMS exchange rate policy: neither fixed rates nor flexibility will fit all circumstances. In some likely situations, it may be desirable all around to defend an existing rate. In other likely cases, flexibility will be useful in counteracting external disturbances or mistaken policies. But the EMS bias appears to be in only one direction, toward what Bryant terms the *minimum variance* view of desirable exchange rate policy.

There was skepticism as well about the flexible character of the EMS design. Despite statements about the readiness to make timely adjustments in currency values, in practice the management of exchange rates by administrative decision may be open to costly delays and errors. The natural tendency of bureaucracies and politicians will be to defer action, as was the case under Bretton Woods. And is it reasonable to expect that when the decision to act is taken the authorities will know by how much to change a given exchange rate? Or may they not make judgments that will either stimulate more exchange market speculation or have unwanted effects on the relative competitive positions of the EMS partners?

Then, too, as optimists and skeptics alike agreed, the workings of the EMS cannot fail to be affected for good or ill by the fortunes of the U.S. dollar. Another flight from dollars into D-marks, in the usual example, could cause severe strains within the EMS as the D-mark rate tended upward. By the same token, a stable dollar would brighten the EMS's prospects for smooth sailing.

The importance of the dollar's position to the fate of the EMS makes obvious the instant need for frequent and full policy consultations between the Community and the United States. If, in the evolution of the EMS, its currency unit (the ECU) were to become a reserve asset alongside the dollar (and perhaps the yen), the requirement for the bilateral or trilateral coordination of policies would have become an imperative of international life. This prospect gives added force to the proposition—which enjoyed common assent at the conference—that the International Monetary Fund's role and authority in international monetary affairs must be preserved. In that connection, the proponents of the EMS stressed that the advent of the new system implied no diminution of support for the IMF and in general dismissed any fears of such a result. The EMS skeptics, though less sanguine, were nevertheless willing to wait and see.

As this introductory sketch suggests and the subsequent text confirms, the conference did not arrive at a consensus, nor was such a result expected or intended. The principal conferees exchanged views among themselves and with the large group of guests that attended the meeting. (It is impracticable, unfortunately, to provide a record of all the exchanges.) This book registers the differences of opinion on the basic points that emerged throughout the dialogue and provides a substantial body of factual and clarifying material on the EMS. Only the course of events will determine whether the EMS will be another failed experiment or a long step toward ultimate European union.

Jacques van Ypersele de Strihou

Operating Principles and Procedures of the European Monetary System

Before analyzing the operating principles and procedures of the European Monetary System, I believe that it is useful to describe some of the motivations behind this effort. I will then discuss the basic principles of the EMS and its conditions for success. Finally, I will try to answer some of the criticisms of the EMS.

Motivations

A principal economic motivation for the creation of the EMS has been dissatisfaction with floating exchange rates during the past few years and the conviction that this monetary situation was having adverse effects on economic integration in Europe and, in general, on growth and employment in the European Community (EC). Expressed in a positive way, the objective of the EMS is to contribute to a lasting improvement of the present economic growth and employment situation of the Community and to its economic integration through greater exchange rate flexibility. This objective will be met only if the system is conceived in such a way that it will be durable and credible and contains neither a deflationary nor an inflationary bias.

Before explaining how the EMS should contribute to growth and employment, let me first talk about greater exchange rate stability. The EMS can help in two ways:
—in a short-term sense, through ironing out excessive fluctuations;
—in the longer term, through fostering greater convergence of the Community economies.

First, the European system, with its intervention rules and credit mechanism, should be able to effectively fight the phenomenon of "overshooting."

5

By this I mean movements of the exchange rate in excess of what would be warranted by differences in inflation rates between countries.

Overshooting has often occurred in the past. It can be initiated by strictly national causes. It can also be initiated—and it often has been—by movements of third currencies, particularly the dollar. When people move out of the dollar because of a lack of confidence in that currency, they do not move equally into all the European currencies. They often move specifically to one EC currency, the deutsche mark. This pushes the D-mark up and it widens the relationships between the D-mark and the French franc or the pound sterling. So one can say that sharp fluctuations of the dollar have also contributed to excessive swings, or overshooting, in European currencies.

Expressing the same idea in the economist's jargon, one can say exchange rates between major currencies have frequently been determined by portfolio adjustments. Such changes have often overshot the purchasing power parity level between these currencies themselves and also between the major currencies and others that are less used as instruments for investments in financial assets. These excessive movements are usually accommodated ex post by price movements, especially in the more open economies, and this tends to exacerbate inflation differentials. The new European exchange rate system, with its provisions for intervention and the available resources to carry out this intervention, should help prevent overshooting.

Second, there is a more fundamental way in which the EMS should contribute to greater exchange rate stability. Participation in this system assumes that in the adjustment process countries will have to give a high priority to internal policy measures rather than rely on exchange rate changes. Otherwise the effectiveness of the system itself would be jeopardized. Participating countries therefore have to realize that, by adhering to this scheme, they compel themselves to aim at greater convergence, through domestic measures, of the fundamentals of their economies. This factor is sometimes called the disciplinary element in the system. But the term should not be misinterpreted. It should not be taken to mean that adjustment is wholly a matter of restrictive policies by deficit countries. Rather the clear intention is that adjustment should take place in a symmetrical way through actions by surplus as well as by deficit countries.

How will greater exchange rate stability contribute to higher growth and employment? There are several ways.

In the first place, it should allow a higher level of both foreign and domestic demand to develop. Monetary instability in Europe has had a deflationary impact in both surplus and deficit countries. In countries with strong currencies, excessive appreciation has contributed to deflationary pressures by reducing profits in export industries and by reducing prospects for sales. This was one of the causes of the downward revisions of growth in Germany in 1977 and 1978.

On the other hand, in countries whose currencies have depreciated too much in relation to stronger currencies, downward overshooting has led to inflationary pressures through increased import prices and wage indexation. These inflationary implications have acted as a brake on economic revival. Governments have been afraid to allow their economies to grow faster lest the expansion increase the pressures on balance of payments and cause further currency depreciation and more inflation.

Thus greater monetary stability should have a positive impact on economic revival by making measures to stimulate higher levels of demand more feasible. This should have important multiplier effects, in view of the openness of EC economies and the high proportion of intra-Community trade in total trade. Trade with other EC partners represents 69 percent of total Belgian trade, between 45 and 50 percent of the trade of France, Germany, Denmark, and Italy, and 38 percent of British trade.

Greater monetary stability would also encourage business confidence and investment. In talks with European business executives, one often hears complaints that they are unable to give their companies a full European dimension because of the ever-present exchange risks and uncertainty about inflation rates. It has been difficult to forecast correctly the cost in national currency of inputs from abroad or the revenue in national currency from exports. These uncertainties contribute to the fact that businesses are not harvesting the potential benefits of a market as large as Europe. Furthermore, they reinforce protectionist pressures and paralyze investment.

In fact, one can safely say that exchange rate fluctuations have in part replaced the old customs barriers in their negative effects on growth and on the development both of a large European market and of enterprises with such a dimension. The dismantling of customs barriers and the progress toward integration contributed to the fast growth in Europe in the 1960s, but the instability of exchange rates between European currencies in the 1970s has been a brake on integration and on growth.

In short, I argue that monetary instability in Europe has had the deflationary bias that some people have wrongly attributed to the EMS design. I will come back to this point later.

Operating Principles and Requirements for Successful Functioning of the EMS

Having analyzed the economic motivation for the creation of the EMS, the main elements of which are described in the appendix to this paper, I will now discuss the operating principles of the EMS and the conditions for its successful functioning. I stress three factors:

—the convergence of underlying economic conditions in the EMS countries;
—flexibility in the operation of the system;
—greater stability between EMS currencies and other currencies.

Convergence of the Community Economies

To be successful, the EMS, first of all, will have to be accompanied by policies designed to achieve a greater convergence of the economies of member states. The EMS cannot be durable and effective unless it is backed by complementary policies. As there are still important divergences in the situations of member states, great effort on the part of all countries and in all areas of policy will be needed if the system is to last.

Unless central rate changes are going to be very frequent, which would in itself limit the usefulness of the EMS, countries must, as noted, in principle give a higher priority to adjustment through internal policy measures than to changes in exchange rates.

Among these efforts, coordination of monetary policies deserves a special role. This is meant to assure a compatibility of the internal monetary objectives of member states with exchange rate objectives and with larger economic objectives. In this framework I believe that attention should be focused more on the coordination of domestic components of money creation, that is, on domestic credit expansion, than on one or more measures of the money stock. It would facilitate the monitoring of the EMS if members would broadly follow the principle of nonsterilization, through open market operations or other means, of exchange-market interventions. This would mean that countries losing reserves would allow tighter money and higher interest rates to reflect the liquidity effects of these losses, as has been the practice of the smaller countries in the "snake." A country facing a temporary accumulation of reserves will also have to remain calm and not try to offset quickly and completely the liquidity effect of sudden inflows of reserves.

Another approach to convergence is through coordination of global demand management policies. The concerted economic action decided upon in Bremen in July 1978, which modulated the extent of expansion of countries according to both balance-of-payments and inflationary problems, was an important approach to convergence. In the Bremen framework the strongest economy (Germany) took expansionary measures. This helped other countries to make necessary adjustments and makes it more probable that the right sort of adjustment and convergence policies will be followed under the EMS. This is one factor that is favorable to the initial functioning of the EMS.

Other elements of domestic policy also have an important role to play. In fact, the immediate issues affecting convergence these days are in the area of incomes policy, particularly in Ireland, Denmark, and Italy, where important wage negotiations are being discussed. The outcome of these negotiations will certainly affect the degree to which convergence can be achieved.

Let me also make a short comment here on the role of the divergence indicator, which is the main novelty in the exchange rate system and which is described more fully in the appendix. When we proposed it, our purpose quite clearly was not only to find a compromise between the two views about what to use as a trigger for mandatory intervention—the parity grid or the European currency unit (ECU)—but also to find an objective indicator as a trigger for policy coordination. This the snake did not have, for it did not indicate who should take measures. Thus the divergence indicator should become one element of a more equilibrated adjustment process and should help induce convergence. It will be very important that all countries make this new element function effectively, as it could be a means of fostering real convergence. Its role is to signal early in the game where divergences are appearing and to induce countries to take corrective actions.

A second condition (in addition to monetary coordination) for successful operation is flexibility in the system. While the EMS by itself should help to reduce differences in inflation rates among countries, it should not prevent remaining significant differences from being reflected in exchange rates. It is necessary to avoid the rigidity of the Bretton Woods system and to "de-dramatize" exchange rate adjustments. Experience in the snake during the last three years has been positive on that score. A number of adjustments have been made, with exchange markets remaining calm. Several of these adjustments involved a general realignment. This was, for instance, the case in the October 1976 snake realignment, which gave new life to the snake when many outside observers were forecasting its imminent death. In a sense, the realignment two years later was also a very successful one. It was a kind of preemptive strike, which anticipated market tensions as the January 1 deadline for the EMS approached. This operation permitted the system to start in a quiet way, first unofficially in January, then officially in March.

If changes in exchange rates can be kept small, it will be an important element in deterring speculation. Often one hears that speculation cannot but gain from a system of stable and adjustable exchange rates. That is not right. To the extent that changes in central rates are smaller than twice the width of the margin of fluctuation it is not at all sure that speculation will gain. If before the change of the central rate a currency is at the floor rate, and after the change is at the ceiling, speculation will not have gained, provided the change in the central rate is smaller than twice the margin.

Experience with the snake has shown that central rates may be adjusted by as much as 4 percent without having much effect on market rates if a depreciating currency manages to shift position with the past strongest currency inside the regular EMS band.

Some commentators on the EMS have criticized it on the ground that it does not provide clear criteria for adjustments of central rates. I disagree. If you set specific criteria for what is to be allowed, you will activate market forces that push you to make those changes. As soon as a country moves toward the indicator, speculation will be triggered. There are many cases in which you might justifiably want to resist a move, even if a sophisticated indicator tells you otherwise. I have often mentioned the case of Belgium in this respect. If Belgium had slavishly followed indicators, it would have been led to adjust in a more significant way vis-à-vis the D-mark in the last few years. Its policy of staying close to the D-mark has allowed it, on the contrary, to rapidly decrease its inflation differential with Germany, from 7 percent in 1975 to less than 0.5 percent in the spring of 1979.

This, of course, is not to say that Belgium does not accept the role of an objective indicator, as is evidenced by its initiative in proposing the divergence indicator. However, this latter indicator can set off different kinds of action, among which I would especially emphasize domestic policy actions. It is true that adjustment in rates is one of the possible actions to be taken, but it is by no means the only one.

Let me now move to a third factor for success of the EMS. A stable relation between the dollar and European currencies is not an absolute condition of success but would greatly contribute to it. Obviously this is an element that is to a large extent outside the direct control of Europeans.

Erratic movements of the dollar have often contributed to the phenomenon of overshooting between European currencies. From this point of view, the smooth start of the EMS has been helped by the relative stability of the dollar. This reflects largely the new and effective concern of the U.S. authorities about the dollar, which has been manifested in monetary and budgetary policies since November 1, 1978. Continuation of such policies by the United States will be helpful to the EMS.

I wonder whether in the future we should not try to formalize somewhat the effort on both sides of the ocean to achieve greater stability. I wonder also whether it would not be feasible to devise a more comprehensive kind of divergence indicator, which would induce a divergent country or regional grouping to take action. Such a divergence indicator could be based on the IMF's special drawing rights. If the dollar, the ECU, or the Japanese yen diverged by a certain percentage against the SDR, this would trigger consultations in which possible action by the divergent country or group of countries would be considered.

Objections

Many criticisms of the EMS have been heard in the Community as well as outside it. I will deal with some of them, realizing fully, however, that the best answers will not come from reasoning in the abstract but rather from the behavior of the new system.

The first and most important objection is that the economic situation in Europe is too divergent to allow a system of stable exchange rates among the European currencies. Those who raise this objection point out that the inflation rates of the nine members of the European Community vary at present between some 3 percent in Germany and 13 percent in Italy. This objection should be examined seriously.

Although comparisons of consumer price indexes are not, in my view, the best criterion for measuring existing inflation differentials, I think the answer to this objection is threefold.

First, it must be recognized that the exchange rate mechanism, if it is the only instrument of coordination, is of limited use. It seems essential that a system intended to stabilize exchange rates must go hand in hand with effective coordination of economic policies, in particular of internal monetary and budgetary policies, but also of incomes policies. It is not so much a question of imposing this convergence from outside. I believe countries have come to realize better in the last few years that it was in their own interests to take domestic measures toward convergence and that floating rates did not in fact grant independence to domestic policy. In other words, one can rightly say that those who adhere to the exchange rate system should be ready to adjust their internal monetary and economic policies accordingly.

Second, agreement on this point, however, does not imply that introduction of the system must wait for a complete disappearance of differences in inflation rates. Action should be taken to reduce them, but they need not be eliminated before the system can become operative. This EMS has sufficient flexibility to allow remaining real disparities to be reflected in exchange rates. In the snake mechanism, it will be noted, divergences have been reflected in changes in exchange rates, changes that have been carried out efficiently during the past few years.

Finally, the EMS includes an element of supplementary flexibility for the member states that did not participate in the snake in 1978. These countries may opt for wider margins (6 percent) around central rates, as Italy has done.

Another objection, partly linked with the first one, says that the system will necessarily be deflationary and will adversely affect employment and economic activity in the Community. The reasoning leading to this conclusion is as follows: those countries with higher inflation rates will be forced to adopt more restrictive monetary, budgetary, and incomes policies, which are detrimental to growth, in order to meet EMS exchange rate objectives.

I cannot agree with this objection, based as it is on what economists call "the Phillips curve," or on an assumption that there is a positive correlation between growth and increases in the price level. This comes down to saying that more inflation is necessary to growth. It is not a proven case. On the contrary, in many cases countries with a low inflation rate but greater confidence have had good rates of growth. The British in recent years have been compelled to recognize the error of this reasoning. Only after the introduction of anti-inflationary monetary, budgetary, and incomes policies did the performance of the British economy improve.

I do not intend to say that there may not be transitional problems for the poorer EC countries in the EMS. Demand management policies may be more difficult to apply in these countries. It is to meet this kind of difficulty that the issue of resource transfers to the poorer countries—Ireland and Italy in particular—has been raised.

The fear that the EMS will have a deflationary bias is also based on the proposition that the D-mark will pull up the other Community currencies above their purchasing power parity and that this will necessarily have deflationary effects through decreased competitiveness. This is an objection that cannot be met in the abstract. It would only be valid if one assumed that the country with a strong currency would refuse to take internal measures to prevent an excessive increase in the value of its currency and would also refuse to have its currency revalued in relation to other currencies. One answer is that the ECU divergence indicator is designed to induce countries whose currency is diverging to take the domestic measures necessary to prevent persistence of the divergence. Furthermore, experience with the snake has already shown that needed changes of the central rates can be carried out efficiently and flexibly.

A third objection is the opposite of the second: that the EMS will have an inflationary bias. Simplified, the reasoning is as follows: differences between inflation rates will continue, and speculation will take place on a large scale. Germany then will be obliged to grant important credits in order to support the weaker currencies. These credits in turn will raise the German money supply and lead to inflationary pressures in that country.

Here again, an answer cannot be given in the abstract. The objection assumes that inflation differentials will remain high and that adequate changes in central rates will be resisted. Let me repeat that a major factor in the efficient functioning of the system will have to be greater effective coordination of economic policies so as to reduce differences in inflation rates. Let me also repeat that, while the EMS itself ought to contribute to reducing divergences in economic performance, it should not prevent remaining real disparities from being reflected in exchange rates. The experience with the snake in the last few years shows that the normal adjustments have not been resisted. There have been periods of heavy intervention to fight speculation, of course, but most of these movements have been reversed within a short time.

Conclusion

An important initiative has been taken in Europe toward greater exchange rate stability. To function successfully, the EMS will have to foster convergence of the economic situations of member countries and be operated in a flexible way.

This initiative should also be seen as an element that can bring greater worldwide monetary stability. In this context the continuance of the recent American efforts to increase the stability of the dollar is an important consideration.

Appendix: Contents of the EMS Agreement

The EMS agreement contains three parts: an exchange rate system; the creation of a European currency, the ECU; and the first steps toward a European Monetary Fund.

The Exchange Rate System

Central rates and intervention rules. Each currency has a central rate related to the ECU. These central rates have been used to establish a grid of bilateral exchange rates around which fluctuation margins of ±2.25 percent are established. EC countries whose currencies did not belong to the snake in December 1978 could opt for wider margins of up to ±6 percent at the outset of the EMS. Italy has availed itself of this opportunity. This wider margin should be gradually reduced as soon as economic conditions permit.

A member state that does not participate in the exchange rate mechanism at the outset—this is the case for the United Kingdom—may participate at a later stage.

Adjustments of central rates will be subject to a common procedure through mutual agreement of all countries participating in the exchange rate mechanism and the Commission of the European Community. When the intervention points defined by the fluctuation margins are reached, intervention in participating currencies is compulsory.

Intervention is also allowed before the margins are reached. In principle, such intervention will also be made in participating currencies, but intervention in third currencies is not excluded. The EMS agreement provides also for "coordination of exchange rate policies vis-à-vis third countries and, as far as possible, a concertation with the money authorities of these countries."

Indicator of divergence. One of the new elements of the EMS that makes it different from the snake, which involves only the parity grid system, is the indicator of divergence. It is a kind of warning system and will signal whether a currency is experiencing a movement differing from the average. The indicator is based on the spread observed between the variable value of the ECU and the ECU numéraire. It flashes when a currency crosses its "threshold of divergence." The formula chosen to calculate this threshold is: 75% × (2.25% or 6%) × (1 less the weight of the currency in the ECU basket). This means that the threshold is set at 75 percent of the maximum spread of divergence allowed for each currency.

The divergence indicator also is calculated so as to eliminate the influence of the weight of each currency on the probability of reaching the threshold. If this had not been done, currencies that have a large weight in the ECU would reach the divergence indicator later than other currencies since they affect the ECU more than the currencies with smaller weights.

Before measuring the effective divergence compared to the threshold, the effective divergence must be adjusted to eliminate the effect of movements of some currencies—the lira and the pound sterling—in excess of 2.25 percent.

Indeed, the lira has a margin of 6 percent and the pound sterling is subject to no margin. This is done so that, for instance, a wide movement of the pound would not by itself lead a currency across its divergence threshold.

When a currency crosses its threshold of divergence, the presumption is that the authorities concerned will correct the situation by adequate measures, such as the following:

—Diversified intervention. This means intervention in various currencies rather than in only the currency that is furthest away from the currency of the intervening country. Diversified interventions allow a better spread of the burden of intervention among currencies of the EMS.

—Measures of domestic monetary policy. This includes, among others, measures affecting the interest rate that have a direct effect on the flow of capital. In the snake system interest rate movements were an important instrument to alleviate tension.

—Changes in central rates. While the EMS itself ought to contribute to reducing divergences in economic performance, it should not prevent remaining real disparities from being reflected in exchange rates.

—Other measures of economic policy. These could include, for instance, changes in budgetary policy or incomes policy.

In case such measures, because of special circumstances, are not taken, the reasons for this shall be given to the other authorities, especially in the "concertation between Central Banks." Consultation will, if necessary, then take place in the appropriate Community bodies, including the Council of Ministers.

After six months, these provisions shall be reviewed in the light of experience.

To summarize this first part, the present EMS differs from the snake, especially in the following ways: (1) membership has been increased by the inclusion of the French franc, the lira, and the Irish pound; (2) one currency has a larger margin, 6 percent, than the standard 2.25 percent; and (3) the system is not only based on a parity grid but also has a new element, the divergence indicator.

The ECU and Its Functions

A European currency unit is at the center of the EMS. The value and the composition of the ECU are identical with the definition of the European unit of account.

The relative weights of the currencies in the ECU were as follows in early March 1979:

Deutsche mark	33.02	Belgian franc	9.23
French franc	19.89	Danish krone	3.10
Pound sterling	13.25	Irish pound	1.11
Dutch guilder	10.56	Luxembourg franc	0.35
Italian lira	9.58		

The ECU will be used (1) as the denominator (numéraire) for the exchange rate mechanism; (2) as the basis for the divergence indicator; (3) as the denominator for operations in both the intervention and the credit mechanisms; (4) as a means of settlement between monetary authorities of the EC.

The weights of currencies in the ECU will be reexamined and if necessary revised within six months of the entry into force of the system and thereafter every five years or, on request, if the weight of any currency has changed by 25 percent. Revisions have to be mutually accepted; they will, by themselves, not modify the external value of the ECU on the day of the change. They will be made in line with underlying economic criteria.

To serve as a means of settlement, an initial supply of ECUs will be provided by the European Monetary Cooperation Fund (EMCF) against the deposit of 20 percent of gold and 20 percent of dollar reserves currently held by central banks. This operation will take the form of specified, revolving swap arrangements. The deposits will be valued in the following ways:

—for gold, whichever of these two prices is lower: the average of the price, converted into ECUs, noted each day at the two fixings in London during the previous six months, or the average of the two fixings noted the day before the last one of the period (so as to avoid a price above the current market value);

—for the dollar, the market rate two days before the date of the deposit.

Every three months, when they renew the swap arrangements, central banks will make the adjustments necessary to maintain deposits with the EMCF corresponding to at least 20 percent of their reserves. This will be done to the extent that their reserves in gold and dollars have changed. The amounts of ECUs issued will also be adjusted according to changes in the market price of gold or in the exchange rate of the dollar.

A member state not participating in the exchange rate mechanism (the United Kingdom) may participate in this initial operation on the basis described.

The European Monetary Fund and Present Credit Mechanisms

The agreement of December 1978 stated:

We remain firmly resolved to consolidate, not later than two years after the start of the scheme, into a final system the provisions and procedures thus created. This system will entail the creation of the European Monetary Fund as announced in the conclusions of the European Council meeting at Bremen on 6/7 July, 1978, as well as the full utilization of the ECU as a reserve asset and a means of settlement. It will be based on adequate legislation at the Community as well as the national level.

In the meantime, existing financing and credit mechanisms will continue, adjusted in the following ways. The very short-term financing facility of an unlimited amount will be continued. Settlements will be made forty-five days after the end of the month of intervention with the possibility of prolongation for another three months for amounts limited to the size of debtor quotas in the short-term monetary support. Under the snake system, settlements had to be made thirty days after the end of the month of intervention. Debtor quotas in the short-term monetary support (which serve as ceiling for the three-month extension privilege) have been multiplied by about 2.5.

The credit mechanisms will be extended to an amount of 25 billion ECUs of effectively available credit. This is about 2.5 times the previous amount. Its distribution will be: for short-term monetary support, 14 billion ECUs; for medium-term financial assistance, 11 billion ECUs.

The substantial increase in the amounts of credit available and the lengthened duration of some credit mechanisms are important elements for strengthening the credibility of the system; they guarantee that, in case of need, large means can be made available to countries to fight speculative movements.

Comments by Ralph C. Bryant

Jacques van Ypersele's paper provides a clear description of the EMS and also a subtle statement covering its rationale, some of the problems it will encounter, and some of the doubts it evokes.

It seems to me I can most usefully focus my comments on the objectives and principles that underlie the EMS initiative. I hope to avoid offering merely an "American" view, and I will not attempt to comment on the possible implications of the EMS for the interests of the United States. Rather I intend to keep mainly to analytical observations about exchange rate variability—to sketch an analytical framework that may help in thinking about the issues raised by the EMS from the perspective of either side of the Atlantic.

As a point of departure, let me summarize the two dominant intellectual approaches to exchange rate variability.

The first may be termed the *untrammeled market position.* It is popular among North American economists and officials but is encountered elsewhere as well. It holds that every nation should pursue appropriate domestic macro-economic policies and then permit currency values to be determined in the foreign exchange market without intervention by central banks or governments.

The second view, most frequently met in Western Europe and Japan, may be labeled the *minimum variance position.* Those holding this view emphasize the uncertainties and disruption that may be associated with exchange rate movements. They argue that governments should act to "maintain as much exchange rate stability as possible." EMS advocates who identify a "zone of monetary stability" in Europe as the prime objective of the experiment appear to take this position, at least for fluctuations of exchange rates between Community currencies.

To provide an analytical framework for evaluating these views about exchange rate variability, imagine an open economy in which external trade is important, banks and nonbanks have significant amounts of assets and liabilities vis-à-vis foreigners, and restrictions on capital flows are not sufficiently comprehensive to prevent shifts in assets when changes occur in expectations about exchange rates, interest rates, or asset prices. Policy actions or nonpolicy disturbances originating abroad have more than trivial effects on the home economy, and vice versa; but typically the effects are greatest in the originating country. In short, suppose the situation of *intermediate interdependence* that actually characterizes Western Europe and North America today.

Make the further, realistic assumption that the primary concern of a nation's policymakers is with national objectives—with levels of employment and prices at home. Little or no welfare value is attached to developments in employment or prices abroad, except as feedbacks are perceived to affect the home economy. Policymakers consider themselves free to adjust the instruments of macroeconomic policy as they deem best. As is the case under the current Articles of Agreement of the IMF, assume that there are no binding supranational constraints on movements of exchange rates and external reserve assets.

How should the home nation's policymakers respond—in particular, should they or should they not allow the exchange rate to move—when various types of nonpolicy disturbances occur?

Consider first a recession that originates abroad, caused by an unexpected increase in the foreign savings rate and an unexpected slump in foreign business investment. That disturbance brings incipient pressure on both the foreign and the domestic economies; market interest rates abroad tend to fall, the domestic currency tends to depreciate, and domestic interest rates tend to fall. Actual adjustments in financial variables depend on how domestic monetary policy is implemented at home and abroad and on the extent, if any, of exchange market intervention.

If the country's central bank chooses to resist its currency's tendency toward depreciation, its external reserve position deteriorates. Exports decline, domestic real output falls, and some downward pressure is exerted on the domestic price level. When the exchange rate is held fixed, the foreign recession is transmitted to the maximum possible extent to the home economy.

If, on the other hand, the domestic currency is allowed to depreciate, the adverse effects of the foreign recession on the home economy are lessened. Domestic output and prices are likely to be lower than they would be if there were no foreign recession, but by smaller amounts than if the exchange rate was held fixed.

Policymakers of the country would thus have reason to reject exchange rate "stability" in these circumstances. Depreciation of the domestic currency, while not desired for its own sake, would help to buffer domestic variables from a disturbance originating outside the home economy.

Consider next a recession that begins at home in response to an unexpected decline in consumption and investment spending by the country's residents. The incipient pressures on financial variables now include tendencies for the home currency to appreciate and for market interest rates to fall at home and abroad.

If the central bank holds the exchange rate stable, external reserves rise. Domestic output and employment fall and prices are under downward pressure. But as imports decline, some of the contractional impetus of the recession is transmitted abroad through the current account of the balance of payments.

If the exchange rate is permitted to appreciate, however, less of the contractional impetus is transferred abroad. Appreciation of the domestic currency tends to reinforce the excess supply created by the initial disturbance in goods markets at home: for example, it causes a fall in import prices relative to those for domestic goods and makes export goods less competitive, thereby leading both indigenous and foreign residents to switch expenditures away from domestic to foreign goods. The disruptive effects of the disturbance are therefore confined more to the home economy because of the appreciation of the domestic currency. From the point of view of the nation's policymakers, exchange rate variability in these circumstances is an inferior alternative to exchange rate stability.

As a third illustrative type of disturbance, consider an unexpected change in asset preferences where private investors, foreign or domestic, decide to increase the proportion of domestic-currency assets in their portfolios. The incipient pressure on financial variables in this case includes tendencies for the home currency to appreciate, for home market interest rates to fall, and for foreign interest rates to rise.

Assuming no central bank intervention in exchange markets causing the domestic currency to appreciate, native and foreign residents switch expenditures away from domestic to foreign goods; imports rise and exports tend to decline. The net result is an unanticipated and unwanted tendency toward contraction in domestic output and prices. (The contractional result is unambiguous if the central bank keeps domestic interest rates from falling while it allows the domestic currency to appreciate.)

If, however, exchange market intervention is carried out to prevent the exchange rate from changing, the external reserves of the country increase but there is no unwanted impact on output and prices (at home or abroad). In effect, the exchange market intervention accommodates the private sector's shift in asset preferences at the existing interest rates and exchange rate by means of offsetting changes in central bank balance sheets.

For this case of an autonomous change in private asset preference, therefore, both the home economy and the foreign economy are better off with exchange market intervention that keeps the exchange rate unchanged.

Analysis of the type sketched out above leads to an eclectic view about exchange rate variability. It shows that the variability of a nation's currency facilitates adjustment to some types of nonpolicy disturbances but aggravates the adverse consequences of others. (An analogous conclusion applies to policy "mistakes"—macroeconomic policy actions that turn out in retrospect to have been undesirable.) Hence it is sometimes desirable for exchange rates to fluctuate. At other times stability is advantageous. As an analytical matter, neither the untrammeled market nor the minimum variance position is sound. It is inappropriate to set either the presence or the absence of exchange rate stability as a goal of national macroeconomic policy. The traditional choice between fixed rates and flexible rates is an artificial one that policymakers do not have to, and should not, make. The proper approach is a discretionary one—managed fixing or managed floating, with "managed" the key word.[1]

With appropriate modifications for the specific circumstances, the framework for analysis that I have outlined can be applied in principle to individual European countries, to the Community or Western Europe as a whole, and to individual non-European economies. It provides a useful background for an

1. The argument summarized here draws on the discussion in part 5 of my forthcoming book, *Money and Monetary Policy in Interdependent Nations.*

inquiry into the prospects for the success or failure of the EMS, especially its planned treatment of variability among the currencies of the Community countries.

In his paper, van Ypersele mentions several motives or objectives for the EMS initiative. He does not differentiate them clearly, nor does he, perhaps understandably, weight them according to their importance. It is illuminating, however, to examine and evaluate them separately.

One objective is to foster exchange rate "stability." Apparently a "zone of monetary stability in Europe" is for some people virtually an end in itself. In any case, avoidance of the discomforts and costs of floating is an important aim, broadly shared by the Community member states.

A second motivation is to facilitate the achievement of national economic goals in the individual EC countries. For example, it is argued that the EMS will make it easier to keep national price levels under control or to promote higher and more stable levels of national employment. One can readily imagine individuals and governments being drawn to the EMS for these national motives without being attracted by the idea of greater European economic integration or political unity.

Finally, a third objective motivates some of the proponents of the EMS: to hasten the economic and political integration of Europe. You may recall that scientific measurement of beauty—the millihelen. One millihelen is the amount of pulchritude needed to launch one ship. It may be that politicians and economists require an analogous scientific measure of progress—genuine progress—toward European integration. Let me offer the "gaullicycle," that is, the amount of progress toward European unity calculated to make Charles de Gaulle turn one full revolution in his grave. One question to ask when evaluating the motives of those Europeans who are ardent supporters of the EMS is, how many gaullicycles do they intend and expect beyond the purely national benefits that are sought?

Conclusions about the likely viability and longevity of the EMS should depend heavily on the balance between these differing motivations and, hence, on the supporting actions that will or will not be taken to advance the several objectives. I will discuss the possibilities by suggesting several hypotheses.

Hypothesis A says that most of the support for the EMS may be ascribed to dissatisfaction with floating exchange rates per se, particularly with the fluctuations between the snake currencies and the dollar. The 1977-78 depreciation of the dollar might then be seen as the mother of the EMS, and the stability of the dollar since November 1978 as the good midwife who assured a smooth birth.

If this hypothesis is correct, one's verdict about the longevity of the EMS would have to be fairly pessimistic. The primary objective of the system is then close to what I have termed the minimum variance position about exchange rate variability. That position does not rest on solid analytical foundations. If fluctuations of the snake currencies against the dollar are viewed as the main difficulty, moreover, the EMS remedy is not suited to the disease it is intended to cure. Stability of exchange rates within Europe can protect against some kinds of disturbances—for example, those having their source in asset markets. But stability, even if it could be maintained, will not protect against other types of disturbance.

Hypothesis B is that support for the EMS is based mainly on the conviction that exchange rate stability—a zone of monetary stability in Europe—will help advance national macroeconomic objectives (for example, anti-inflationary policies). The emphasis here is less on the dollar's fluctuations against snake currencies than on the alleged positive gains to European economies from stability among European currencies themselves.

Despite the difference in emphasis, this view is again close to the minimum variance position about exchange rates. It is similarly liable to periodic frustration. The situations and interests of the European nations are so divergent that economic disturbances may often create circumstances in which it is preferable for some European nations to hold exchange rates steady and for others to let them vary. Could one think, for instance, that it would be in the interests of both Germany and France to deal with a wage explosion in France by intervention to stabilize the deutsche mark-franc exchange rate?

Under the first two hypotheses, it would be appropriate to interpret the initiation of the EMS as an experiment little different from earlier efforts at European monetary unification. The EMS would be based on views that are no more durable than those incorporated in the earlier Barre and Werner reports or in the agreement establishing the snake in the tunnel. A temporary convergence of short-run national interests in promoting exchange rate stability under "fair weather" conditions would disguise fundamental differences in national interests. With such shaky foundations, the EMS would be likely to run into trouble in future years when the weather was stormy.

Hypothesis C asserts that the primary aim of the EMS is to facilitate better achievement of national macroeconomic objectives, but to do so through more "ordered management" of exchange rates, including exchange rate changes among Community currencies as may be desirable from time to time. If this hypothesis is correct, the EMS still represents a negligible number of gaulli-cycles toward greater European integration. Unlike hypotheses A and B, however, this approach is not based on the minimum variance position about exchange rate variability. If orderly, prompt changes in the EMS parity grid are indeed going to take place when needed, one's judgment about the likely durability and longevity of the EMS can be more favorable. The system will emphasize not a particular set of exchange rates, but rather the pragmatic management of intra-European exchange rate variability. Note that under this hypothesis the zone of monetary stability becomes a much subordinated objective of the Community.

Now assume, contrary to the preceding hypotheses, that the hope for greater progress toward European integration is a major driving force behind the EMS experiment. If that assumption is true, one can presume that when the economic or political interests of an individual EC nation conflict with the interests of others or the Community as a whole (as will happen) that nation will be willing to sacrifice its national goals to a greater extent than in the past. Not only in fair weather but also in foul, the interests of the Community as a whole are to move up the scale of priorities relative to national interests.

Hypothesis D is one variant of the view that "integration" should get a higher priority than in the past. It asserts that the "Europeanist" strategy, often attributed to Jean Monnet, lies behind the creation of the EMS. That strategy, you recall, relies on an apparently technical initiative in the monetary field to catalyze greater integration. But it does not simultaneously involve direct steps to foster greater convergence in nations' domestic macroeconomic policies.

A zone of monetary stability within Europe—if that indeed meant unchanging exchange rates regardless of national objectives—would of course force more integration by requiring a convergence of domestic policies. But substantial differences still exist among European nations—in the ultimate goals of their economic policies, in their experiences with internal nonpolicy disturbances, in the behavior patterns of their residents, and in their institutional, social, and legal environments. If European policymakers seek to bring about greater integration among their heterogeneous economies solely by trying to stabilize their currencies vis-à-vis each other, the attempt seems certain to be abortive. So long as the more basic differences in national objectives, behavior patterns, and institutions remain, the means (exchange rate stability) will have to be abandoned long before the end (greater integration) has been accomplished.

That brings me to a final hypothesis E, which supposes not only that the Community nations now intend to give European integration a high political priority, but also that they plan to institute a number of complementary direct measures to bring about a convergence of domestic economic policies. This will call for a large number of gaullicycles of progress, both in the intent of policymakers and in their success in carrying out their intentions. If this ambitious agenda is attempted, the prognosis for the EMS should be very different from the prognoses under the other hypotheses. If the political will were to be strong enough to forcefully promote a much greater convergence of national policies, one could reasonably foresee progress toward genuine integration and, following from it, good prospects for exchange rate stability.

For purposes of this discussion I have sharply differentiated the possible objectives for and motivations behind the EMS. In practice, of course, they are intermingled. I, for one, am not clear about how to weight them. I suspect that the several founders of the EMS give them substantially different weights. I am therefore led to conclude with an agnostic judgment, which may be encapsulated in two contradictory aphorisms attributed to English scholars.

On the one hand, the EMS seems to warrant the verdict of Samuel Johnson on second marriages. "A second marriage," said Johnson, "is the triumph of hope over experience." For the lira, the EMS represents a second marriage; for the French franc, it is a third.

On the other hand, it is conceivable that the time has arrived for new political moves toward European unity. It may even be the case that new efforts will be made, in association with the operation of the EMS, to promote a genuine convergence of domestic macroeconomic policies. In that case, the appropriate aphorism is the remark made to a young woman by the classical scholar and master of Balliol College, Oxford, Benjamin Jowett. "You must believe in God, my dear," Jowett said, "despite what the clergymen say."

It thus seems prudent to leave the issue open. Skepticism about the EMS is easy to justify. But, just possibly, one should believe in its viability despite what the economists say.

Michael Emerson

The European Monetary System in the Broader Setting of the Community's Economic and Political Development

In this paper I discuss the European Monetary System as it relates to the outlook for the Community's progress more generally. (I will not deal with the monetary mechanisms of the EMS, which are treated in other papers.)

Commentators are offering a wide range of interpretations of the EMS, from its being, on the one hand, a strategic catalyst in the Community's economic and political integration to its being, on the other hand, a relapse into the doomed world of pre-Smithsonian fixed exchange rates. My argument is that it belongs in the former category, and that it is more than the manifestation of ECUmenical spirit in monetary matters (noted approvingly by Henry Reuss in a recent lecture).

Curiously, perhaps, the Treaty of Rome prescribed most of the factors necessary for monetary integration but without setting monetary union as an objective. For in general one would expect monetary integration, and ultimately union, to become a proposition relatively advantageous to a region that has a high degree of trade interdependence and of capital and labor mobility; a region that is politically homogeneous enough to devolve to common institutions powers of directly applicable legislation; a region that, for example, decides after some twenty years of Common Market experience to proceed with the creation of a directly elected parliament to make the link between the common institutions and the people. Since these are the fundamentals of the integration process, it is worthwhile examining what the realities and recent trends have been beneath the simple headings. Is the Community really integrating, and how is the process affected by the EMS?

Trade

When the Community began in 1958 its member states (at present nine) sold 34 percent of their total exports to other member states.[1] That ratio had risen to 52 percent by 1976 (see table 1). There is a similar ratio on the import side (table 2). If one also includes other European countries in the Organization for Economic Cooperation and Development, the Community's total intra-European exports rose to 67 percent of total exports, or 19 percent of Community GDP. (Of the other European countries, all have either applied to join the Community or are linked to the Community by special trade or association agreements.)

The Community's merchandise exports (excluding services) to other continents amounted to 12 percent of GDP in 1977. By comparison, in the same year U.S. exports outside North America amounted to 5.5 percent of GDP, and Japan's total exports amounted to 11.5 percent of its GDP. Thus while the Community's trade structure is to a high degree *intra*continental, the extent of its *inter*continental export trade is twice that of the United States, and about equivalent to Japan's total export trade dependence.

Among the original six member states there are signs of a leveling off in the fraction of GDP devoted to intra-Community trade. The intra-Community exports of Germany, France, and Italy appear to have stabilized at around 10 percent of GDP for several years. Meanwhile the United Kingdom's sales to the Community have risen rapidly, from 4.7 percent of GDP in 1972, the last year before joining, to 8.6 percent in 1978. The share of intra-Community trade in total exports dipped a little in 1974, the year of fastest growth of OPEC imports, but this was reversed in 1976 (in terms of percentage shares of total trade).

While it may be of little more than academic interest, one can note that the preponderance of Europe's intracontinental trade has been remarkably stable for the past 150 years. It has been estimated that intracontinental exports accounted for 72 percent of total European exports in 1930, 68 percent in 1860, 72 percent in 1880, 68 percent in 1910, 64 percent in 1938, and 74 percent in 1970.[2] Only the United Kingdom, among European countries,

1. Most of the data given in this text are from Commission of the European Communities, "Annual Economic Review 1978-79," *European Economy* (Brussels), no. 1 (November 1978).

2. The historical trade data for the years 1830 to 1970 are from Paul Bairoch, "Geographical Structure and Trade Balance of European Foreign Trade from 1800 to 1970," *Journal of European Economic History* (Banco di Roma), vol. 3 (Winter 1974). Bairoch's data for 1970 are not exactly comparable with those given in table 1.

Table 1. Structure of European Community Exports, by Country and Region, 1958 and 1976

Percent

Exports of to	DK 1958	DK 1976	D 1958	D 1976	F 1958	F 1976	IRL 1958	IRL 1976	I 1958	I 1976	NL 1958	NL 1976	BLEU 1958	BLEU 1976	UK 1958	UK 1976	EC 1958	EC 1976
DK			2,96	2,59	0,75	0,79	0,05	0,63	0,77	0,85	2,63	1,72	1,64	1,44	2,37	2,55	2,00	1,77
D	20,05	14,60			10,46	17,28	2,22	8,78	14,29	19,19	18,98	31,46	17,57	23,42	4,20	7,15	6,71	12,82
F	2,97	4,17	7,58	13,15			0,79	5,18	5,31	15,24	4,87	10,82	10,60	21,17	2,42	6,67	4,59	10,38
IRL	0,30	0,42	0,25	0,27	0,16	0,32			0,13	0,24	0,45	0,38	3,50	0,27	3,50	4,86	1,16	0,94
I	5,31	4,50	5,02	7,42	3,37	10,89	0,43	2,34			2,74	5,25	2,27	4,77	2,11	3,22	3,08	5,92
NL	2,19	3,19	8,10	9,71	2,03	5,10	0,51	5,98	2,05	4,14			20,70	17,07	3,14	5,85	5,41	7,07
BLEU	1,24	1,68	5,69	7,92	6,34	10,16	0,80	4,55	2,27	3,91	14,97	15,58			1,93	5,46	4,89	7,43
UK	25,91	17,11	3,95	7,76	4,89	6,03	78,76	49,42	6,83	4,86	11,90	8,45	5,71	6,07			5,72	5,69
Total intra-Community trade	57,92	45,70	34,49	45,85	27,98	50,61	83,54	76,92	31,64	48,47	56,53	73,69	52,81	74,25	19,64	35,78	34,28	52,08
Other European OECD-countries	17,58	29,53	25,17	19,82	11,14	12,23	1,87	4,45	18,69	13,68	13,19	9,15	11,07	18,02	10,31	15,64	15,46	14,88
USA	9,34	5,83	7,31	5,63	5,93	4,52	5,85	7,01	9,71	6,55	5,64	2,89	9,42	3,57	8,83	9,60	7,79	5,59
Canada	0,68	0,78	1,19	0,78	0,83	0,78	0,67	1,13	1,19	0,96	0,79	0,37	1,13	0,36	5,77	2,45	2,34	0,59
Japan	0,20	1,41	0,95	1,09	0,32	0,75	0,05	1,28	0,32	0,87	0,41	0,48	0,60	1,40	0,61	1,40	0,59	0,93
Australia	0,26	0,42	1,02	0,69	0,46	0,27	0,08	0,97	0,79	0,70	0,68	0,41	0,55	0,29	7,11	2,68	2,50	0,82
Developing countries	9,65	12,50	22,30	17,85	48,38	24,17	1,57	7,29	27,86	21,86	18,14	10,58	18,80	9,86	33,81	25,97	28,49	18,61
of which: OPEC		4,19		8,10		9,11		3,48		11,63		4,36		4,02		11,16		8,09
Other developing countries		8,31		9,75		15,06		3,81		10,23		6,22		5,84		14,81		10,52
Centrally planned economies	3,80	3,56	5,00	6,90	3,70	5,76	0,21	0,64	4,69	5,96	1,98	2,15	3,75	2,64	3,09	3,00	3,75	4,88
Rest-world and unspecified	0,61	0,69	2,62	1,39	1,27	0,91	6,19	0,31	4,99	0,95	2,68	0,28	1,90	0,47	10,87	3,48	4,79	1,26
World (excl. EEC)	42,08	54,30	65,51	54,15	72,02	49,39	16,46	23,08	68,36	51,53	43,47	26,31	47,19	27,75	80,36	64,22	65,72	47,92
World (incl. EEC)	100	100	100	100	100	100	100	100	100	100	100	100	100	100	100	100	100	100

Source: *European Economy*, no. 1 (November 1978).

Key to abbreviations: DK, Denmark; D, West Germany; F, France; IRL, Ireland; I, Italy; NL, the Netherlands; BLEU, Belgium–Luxembourg Economic Union; UK, United Kingdom; EEC, European Economic Community.

Table 2. Structure of European Community Imports, by Country and Region, 1958 and 1976

Percent

Imports of → / to	DK 1958	DK 1976	D 1958	D 1976	F 1958	F 1976	IRL 1958	IRL 1976	I 1958	I 1976	NL 1958	NL 1976	BLEU 1958	BLEU 1976	UK 1958	UK 1976	EC 1958	EC 1976
DK			3,35	1,50	0,63	0,61	0,70	0,87	2,19	0,89	0,67	0,74	0,53	0,45	3,07	2,20	2,04	1,11
D	19,84	20,85			11,64	19,21	4,00	6,88	12,13	16,97	19,48	23,78	17,16	22,39	3,60	8,60	8,33	13,05
F	3,43	3,80	7,59	11,63			1,60	4,70	4,86	13,55	2,79	6,93	11,60	16,26	2,67	6,63	4,29	8,46
IRL	0,01	0,17	0,10	0,36	0,05	0,28			0,05	0,21	0,05	0,40	0,10	0,40	2,90	2,76	0,91	0,71
I	1,70	2,84	8,03	8,51	2,35	8,92	0,85	2,55			1,77	3,33	2,15	3,82	2,04	3,59	2,57	5,34
NL	7,34	5,48	4,53	13,77	2,53	6,08	2,86	3,18	2,58	4,70			15,72	17,59	4,22	5,45	5,29	8,19
BLEU	3,81	3,84	4,38	8,60	5,37	9,59	1,83	1,94	2,02	3,68	17,85	13,98			1,61	2,99	4,46	6,73
UK	22,82	10,22	5,43	3,85	3,59	4,90	56,41	49,27	5,50	3,50	7,39	6,12	7,40	6,73			5,14	4,72
Total intra-Community trade	58,92	47,18	33,41	48,20	26,13	49,55	68,21	69,38	29,30	43,47	49,97	55,25	54,63	67,63	20,09	32,20	33,00	48,16
Other European OECD-countries	19,51	26,70	17,55	12,16	8,55	8,82	4,43	5,40	12,50	8,04	7,84	6,43	8,19	5,64	14,11	12,04	12,69	9,97
USA	9,10	5,15	13,57	7,91	10,04	7,33	6,98	8,55	16,23	7,88	11,31	9,06	9,92	6,12	9,34	11,37	11,16	8,22
Canada	0,25	0,38	3,10	1,05	1,02	0,95	2,97	1,29	1,44	1,30	1,43	0,69	1,42	1,04	8,17	3,63	3,71	1,42
Japan	1,48	2,88	0,61	2,45	0,18	1,91	1,07	2,22	0,41	1,35	0,82	1,58	0,63	1,58	0,94	2,74	0,69	2,08
Australia	0,03	0,09	1,21	0,70	2,42	0,72	1,21	0,15	3,01	0,90	0,20	0,31	1,73	0,59	5,40	1,25	2,71	0,73
Developing countries	6,06	12,14	24,43	20,44	46,71	26,26	9,67	8,58	31,18	28,19	25,02	23,54	19,50	14,51	34,98	25,80	30,41	22,70
of which:																		
OPEC		5,40		10,23		17,71		4,10		18,42		15,76		7,44		13,84		13,56
Other developing countries		6,74		10,21		8,55		4,48		9,77		7,78		7,07		11,96		9,17
Centrally planned economies	4,59	4,85	5,31	4,97	3,30	3,48	1,24	2,37	3,60	6,09	2,61	2,61	2,01	1,85	3,19	3,78	3,55	4,01
Rest-world and unspecified	2,17	0,63	0,84	2,12	1,68	0,98	4,26	2,06	2,36	2,78	1,73	0,50	1,73	1,04	3,82	7,20	2,28	2,71
World (excl. EEC)	41,08	52,82	66,59	51,80	73,87	50,45	31,79	30,62	70,70	56,53	50,03	44,75	45,37	32,37	79,91	67,80	67,00	51,73
World (incl. EEC)	100	100	100	100	100	100	100	100	100	100	100	100	100	100	100	100	100	100

Source: Same as table 1.

has ever had a preponderance of non-European trade. British exports to Europe were about 35 percent of its total exports for most of the century from 1860 to 1960—almost exactly half the degree of European trade dependence of the rest of Europe. The proportion has risen to 51 percent and is still rising.

If trade interdependence were the only criterion for determining membership in a monetary integration club, one should not be surprised at what has happened: a strong interest in European monetary integration on the part of most of Europe, with the United Kingdom remaining somewhat apart but at the same time not wishing to be detached from a movement of great potential significance for the future.

Will the EMS give a new boost to trade integration? The presumption and intention is yes. Of course, one cannot be precise in answering such questions. However, the opinions of businessmen and employers' organizations are affirmative. Exchange risks have in recent years been a deterrent, for example, to firms that must decide whether to make investments in marketing efforts across Europe as well as in increased production capacity. Two types of beneficial effect are thus sought from the EMS, a trade-deepening effect and a general tonic for investors' confidence, the latter implying an improvement in the responsiveness of the real economy to demand management policy.

Labor and People

The free movement of labor is a hallmark of integration. It is a matter of principle, of personal rights and liberties, in any political union. It also profoundly affects the processes of economic adjustment in an economic and monetary union.

All nationals of member states have the unconditional right to seek employment in other member states. When a job is obtained, the migrant is automatically entitled to a residence permit for five years, which is renewable, also automatically, for periods of five years. This applies equally to members of the family (children, parents).

To persons not seeking employment (retired persons or anybody else), the above provisions have not so far applied; such persons are required to obey normal residence regulations for foreigners. However, on this important question new proposals are about to be made by the EC Commission, following an initiative by the European Council in 1974 and more recently by the European Parliament in a resolution of 1977. The new proposals would cover all categories of persons not covered under the arrangements for employed (or self-employed) persons and would give them equivalent rights provided they

could show that they would not be a charge on the social security system of
the host country. These new proposals, if legislated, could have a notable legal
and public opinion impact in no longer classifying Community nationals as
"foreigners" when they are in other EC countries.

The only category of employment for which all Community nationals have
not up until now had equal rights is the protected professions (medicine, law,
and so on). Here, however, there is considerable movement in Community
legislation. One by one, these professions are being brought under the terms
of Community directives that determine rights to establish practices across
Community frontiers: doctors in 1976, advocates in 1977, dentists in 1980,
nurses in 1979, veterinaries in 1981. Architects, midwives, engineers, accoun-
tants, and tax advisers are in the pipeline.

The macroeconomic aspect of labor mobility has so far hardly been an
issue between the member states. Table 3 shows that the numbers of people

**Table 3. Labor Migration in the European Community: Foreign Employees
in Member States, by Nationality, 1976**

Country	Nationals working in other member states (thousands)	Domestic working population (thousands)	Nationals working in other member states as a percentage of domestic working population
Belgium	68	3,713	1.8
Denmark	7	2,293	0.2
Germany	137	24,556	0.5
France	114	20,836	0.5
Ireland	455	1,021	44.6
Italy	694	18,930	3.6
Luxembourg	6	148	4.1
Netherlands	83	4,542	1.8
United Kingdom	61	24,425	0.2
Total, EC	1,625	100,568	1.6
Spain	447	12,535	3.5
Greece	239	3,230	7.4
Portugal	569	3,279	17.4
Turkey	587	14,710	4.0
Yugoslavia	458	...	...
Algeria	447	...	...
Morocco	183	...	...
Tunisia	85	...	...
Other countries	1,392	...	...
Total, non-EC	4,407	...	...
Total	6,032	...	...

Source: Staff of the Commission of the European Communities.

involved have been quite small. In the Community as a whole, migrant workers from other Community countries amount to only 1.6 percent of the working population. It seems that there is a certain minimum amount of labor migration involved in the normal course of commercial and social integration. Thus 0.5 percent of the working population of both France and Germany work in other Community countries; the ratio is higher, as one would expect, for the smaller, open economies—1.8 percent each for Belgium and the Netherlands. Migration from these four countries could be called "pure integration migration," as distinct from "structural migration" from less prosperous to more prosperous areas. It seems that pure integration migration is on the increase although the numbers are quite small. Migration from the five original member countries (excluding Italy) increased from 22,000 new arrivals a year in the period 1958-70 to 31,000 a year in 1971-76. But structural migration has been declining. Italian arrivals dropped from an annual average of 171,000 in 1958-70 to 43,000 in 1973-76. Net emigration from Ireland has practically ceased. Denmark and the United Kingdom still have a relatively low fraction of their domestic working population elsewhere in the Community (0.2 percent). The high Irish figure (44.6 percent) of course reflects generations of Anglo-Irish history.

Enlargement of the Community to include Greece, Spain, and Portugal raises more important issues of structural migration. Already these three countries have over 1.2 million nationals employed in the Community; other Mediterranean nonapplicant countries have 1.6 million nationals employed in the Community. Since 1974 immigration from these countries has been restricted. In the case of the Greek enlargement negotiations a seven-year transitional period will apply before all controls are removed; in the meantime Greek nationals will be accorded a priority status in member states' labor market policies toward foreign employees.

Looking ahead, it seems certain that the Community will retain a relatively low propensity for internal migration because of language and cultural barriers, but will continue to support the individual's right to work and live in the area of his choice. By comparison with the United States this means that migration is likely to feature less in the adjustment of economic imbalances between regions and member states. The major immediate concern is to prevent a further depopulation of the applicant member countries and the Italian south. The example of Ireland is encouraging: it has switched from being a country of structural emigration to one of rapid domestic development. Community policy toward the applicant member state will favor a strong regional development effort in those countries. The prospect of a Community "sun-belt" development in the Mediterranean countries may even feature in some end-of-millennium scenarios. But this is more likely to concern retired people (as in Florida) than the wholesale transplantation of all social categories from north to south. The stability of exchange rates is of major concern to retired northern Europeans on fixed incomes when deciding whether they can risk going to live in the sun.

A low propensity for the individual to migrate means that he may accept relatively large cross-frontier income differentials. Thus it will take a particularly large income gain to persuade a Community national to migrate across a language and cultural frontier. This factor alone supports the proposition that the exchange rate can still be effective in Europe as an instrument of economic adjustment. On the other hand, trade unions are paying more attention to income parity across frontiers in Europe, as is beginning to be manifested in pay negotiations of some major multinationals (the American automobile companies supply leading examples with highly integrated plants in the "golden triangle" of the Rhineland-Ruhr, Benelux, northeast France, and southeast England). Moreover, the country in the middle of this group is Belgium, whose economy operates one of the most comprehensive wage-price indexation systems. These latter factors work against exchange rate adjustments.

In addition, there is the case of cross-frontier commuters, as opposed to migrants. Substantial numbers of people living near the French-German-Benelux frontiers commute daily across these frontiers and are prepared to switch their country of employment according to short-term exchange rate changes. Exchange rate instability is extremely detrimental to the steady economic development of these regions; the EMS should help them.

Overall, the links between the EMS and the Community's policies and preferences regarding the movement of labor are rather complex. The EMS certainly does not seek to prevent exchange rate adjustments where these are necessary. The relative immobility of labor in principle leaves scope for such adjustments to work, although this is impaired by wage indexation practices. Cultural and political values at national and regional levels also mean that there will be a strong preference for adjustment through regional development backed by national and Community resource transfers rather than migration; and the pressure for regional resource transfers will be greater if exchange rate adjustments work ineffectively—and vice versa. Greater exchange rate stability could induce more migration of retired persons; and it is highly desirable for regions where cross-frontier commuting is important. Finally, the EMS, as a new spur to the Community integration process, seems likely to stimulate a wide range of micromeasures that will make it easier for the individual to work, live, and travel across frontiers.

Capital

Capital movement liberalization in the Community is considerable, but incomplete. Capital movements are almost completely liberalized in the countries whose currencies have been strongest—Germany and the Benelux countries (though Belgium has retained a double exchange market for current and capital transactions). Denmark, France, Ireland, Italy, and the United Kingdom retain certain restrictions, which have been authorized by the EC Commission as safeguards for the balance of payments (under article 108 or 109 of the Treaty of Rome). The procedure is that the EC Commission makes periodic examinations of the case for maintaining such restrictions. The next such review will be carried out by the end of September 1979.

Existing restrictions are as follows. Denmark's restrictions are on portfolio investments, but outward investments into bonds issued by the Community and certain international organizations are exempt. France's restrictions in principle cover a wide range of capital transactions, but in practice several categories have been wholly or largely liberalized. Italy requires bank deposits of a fraction of the value of outward portfolio and real estate investments. The United Kingdom retains controls over direct, portfolio, and personal capital movements, but there were relaxations in 1977, including some preferential arrangements with respect to the Community (personal capital movements for migrants to other member states, Community bond issues). Ireland's exchange control regime has been affected by the EMS. In December 1978 Ireland decided to apply to the United Kingdom the same regime as for other member states although the United Kingdom provisionally maintained its existing liberalized regime toward Ireland.

In general there was no desire during the EMS negotiations to add new uncertainties (such as exchange control changes) to the markets or further complexities to the negotiations beyond minimal adjustments to the Irish-British exchange control frontier. The EC Commission's policy is to pursue a progressive dismantling of the remaining restrictions.

The Community is increasing its own capital market operations. It now has five borrowing and lending facilities. The European Coal and Steel Community and the European Investment Bank are the oldest. In 1975 an EC borrowing facility was created for recycling petrodollars to member states in balance-of-payments difficulty. In 1978 Euratom began to borrow and lend for the financing of nuclear power stations. In 1978 a new EC investment financing power (known as the "Ortoli facility") was agreed upon with a view to aiding Community policies in such areas as energy, transport infrastructure, regional development, and industrial reconversion. Also in 1978 it was decided to double the capital of the European Investment Bank. The bank will also act as agent on the project expenditure side of the Ortoli facility. Total gross borrowing under these facilities has risen over the last six years from under 500 million European units of account (EUA) in 1970-72 to 2.5 billion to 3 billion EUA in 1976-78, thus occupying a significant place in international bond markets. With recent increases in the range of borrowing powers, the Community is now better equipped to support a number of its structural policies; moreover these instruments also proved useful in the EMS negotiations (as explained further below), thus making the link between the Community's structural microeconomic instruments and its macroeconomic policies. The idea of ECU-denominated bonds by the Community institutions and national authorities has also been debated by a number of official Community personalities.

Convergence

This word, as far as I know, does not appear in the 1,500 pages of the Treaty of Rome and allied texts. But it is now one of the most often used words in current statements of Community policy. Convergence applies to economic policy and performance.

The Community's foundation and first years of activity concerned above all the three freedoms of trade, labor, and capital movement. The Community's action was essentially through legislation, either by the direct application of Community law (regulations) or by the harmonization of national legislation (according to directives).

The idea of convergence is perhaps the touchstone of the Community's present second generation of activity. Community progress is now less a matter of legislation and enforcement than of economic performance and assessment; but it is no less fundamental for that.

The EMS focuses attention first and foremost on the convergence of inflation rates and a lower dispersion of rates around this average. Figure 1 shows the performance of member states since 1958. The average consumer price rise in the Community (of the present nine members) was 3.3 percent in 1958-68. In 1975, at the height of the instability following the oil crisis, it

Figure 1. Convergence and Divergence of Inflation Rates (Consumer Prices) in Relation to the Community Average (A) and the Most Stable Member State (B)

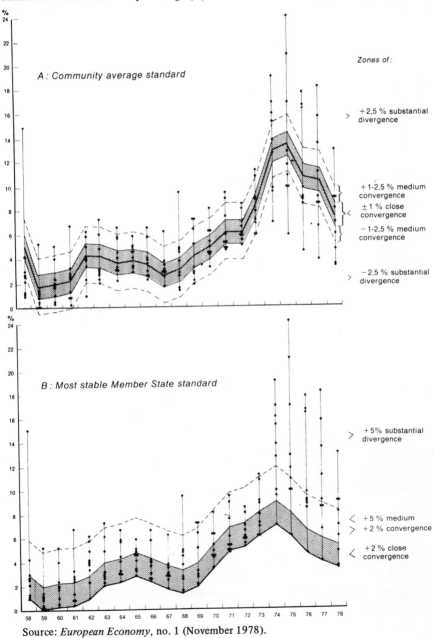

Source: *European Economy*, no. 1 (November 1978).

rose to 13.4 percent, and then declined to 7 percent in 1978. The dispersion of inflation rates, measured by the standard deviation of consumer price rises, was about 1.5 percent in the 1960s; it rose to over 5 percent in 1975, and declined to just under 3 percent in 1978.

From this, may one conclude that the performance of the 1960s would be adequate for a soundly functioning EMS, even if the Bretton Woods system collapsed at the end of that period? The snake has worked reasonably smoothly with larger inflation differentials (between Germany, Benelux, and Denmark) than in the 1960s with the aid of periodic small parity adjustments; and the collapse of global fixity occurred for other reasons. The Community's problem is not so much whether the standards of the 1960s would be adequate, but whether they are approximately attainable. The year 1979 will certainly be a more difficult one in which to continue the progress achieved since 1975, in part because of the new oil price rises. The Benelux countries seem to have consolidated a low rate of inflation, within one point of Germany's. Denmark's inflation rate has now come down to under 7 percent after a long period of double-digit inflation. France's inflation rate has decelerated only slowly, but here it must be remembered that the process of disinflation is being run concurrently with the decontrol of prices and desubsidization of public sector tariffs; the latter moves are seen as a convergence of microeconomic or supply management policy closer to the German example.

In other countries—Ireland, Italy, and the United Kingdom—major income negotiations now under way will largely determine whether recent progress in reducing inflation can be conserved and improved upon. In general terms, in these and other member states, it is arguable that there has been a considerable convergence in economic thinking in recent years. Certainly the idea, once dear to economic analysis, that all countries exhibited stable but different inflation-employment trade-offs has been largely discredited. Hardly any politician, economist, employer, or trade unionist can be heard arguing that higher employment could now be bought with higher inflation, except possibly for a matter of months. In debate on the implications of European monetary integration, conflict over alleged differences in the degree of preoccupation with unemployment has been relatively minor.

Perceptions of the (limited) capacity of demand management policy to reduce unemployment have notably converged—even in the course of the past year. The tendencies in some quarters in Germany toward extreme demand management pessimism have been attenuated by the positive experience of engineering in 1978 and 1979 a concerted upswing in the European economy. The contrary tendencies toward extreme demand management optimism in the United Kingdom have been attenuated by experience of the swift reaction of financial markets to policy moves at the end of the margin for maneuver. In Italy recent experience has shown that very large movements of public finance do not necessarily determine at all tightly the behavior of the private economy. Correspondingly, in the domain of monetary policy there has been a higher degree of consensus in thinking—as has perhaps been the case world-wide. The four major countries have recently aimed at the control of money or credit aggregates, with some secondary convergence for 1979 in the technical design of targets. The EMS, of course, somewhat changes the environment for domestic monetary policy, for example, in the relative appropriateness of money supply as compared to domestic credit targets, and thought is being given to these issues.

The Community's concept of convergence is not limited to stabilization policy. The reduction of regional disparities is a fundamental objective of the Community, written into the Treaty of Rome. But the idea of regional policy in a narrow sense has tended to give way to the idea that the Community's various sectoral policies and financial instruments should be addressed consistently to the objective of achieving more convergent levels of economic performance—as may be seen in the texts of the conclusions of the several meetings of the European Council.

On the measurement and analysis of "real" economic convergence, inter-country comparisons have long been confused by the erratic and misleading guidance offered by data based on market exchange rates. The EC Commission has now begun publishing national accounts data based on purchasing power parities. The story told by these data is summarized in figure 2. While the more familiar market exchange rate data show a sharp widening of per capita GDP differentials between member states from 1960 to 1976, the purchasing power parity data show a slight narrowing of the extreme differences. It also seems that differences in regional product per capita between the regions within the four larger member states declined slightly over the period 1970-75 when suitable measures of interregional inequality are used.[3] Rough comparisons between the Community and the United States can be made. In 1975 the mini-max ratio in personal income per capita of the richest and poorest regions in the United States was 1.4 at the level of nine regions, or 2.9 at the level of fifty states. In the Community the most comparable figures were 2.2 at the level of nine member states and 4.0 at the level of seventy-two

3. The data on regional income per capita are taken from Sir D. Magdougall and others, *Role of Public Finance in European Integration,* vol. 1 (Brussels: Commission of the European Communities, 1977).

Figure 2. Dispersion of Gross Domestic Product per Capita, 1960 and 1976

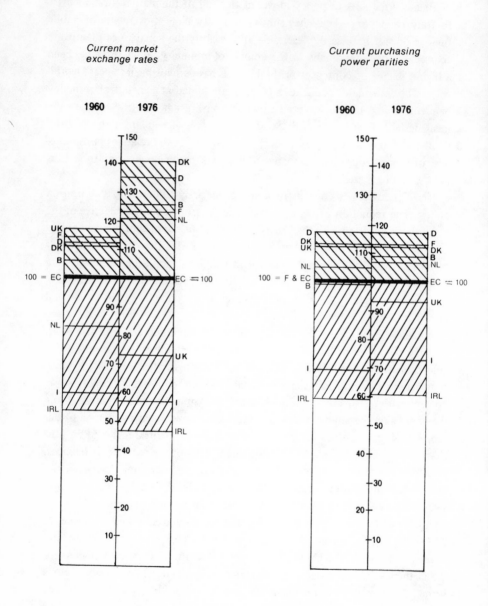

Source: Same as figure 1.

regions—these Community ratios are measured at purchasing power parity exchange rates. The statistically superior (but less familiar and transparent) Gini coefficients tell a similar story, which is that Community regional income differentials are certainly wider than those found in the United States but not by an incomparably larger margin, particularly if one bears in mind the Community's still small instruments of regional policy and the language and cultural frontiers.

The performance of member states may be summarized as follows. Six countries—Germany, France, Benelux, and Denmark—are in more or less the same bracket of income and productivity levels. Of the other member states, as noted, Ireland is changing its economic structure fastest.

The idea of convergence includes that of a stable pattern of balance of payments. Most attempts to define at all closely a normative set of current account balances, or indeed of any other balances, have foundered. However, it is significant that the EMS is starting at a time when none of the four largest member states are facing balance-of-payments constraints. The Benelux countries are no longer in surplus, but they are not in difficulty; the large deficits on current account of goods and services of Ireland and Denmark are being financed in sustainable ways—including official transfers from the Community and long-term capital inflows.

Factors that should make for greater convergence along these lines are (1) shifts in broad economic policy attitudes, notably in stabilization policy and (as important, but hardly discussed in this paper) resource allocation policy; (2) the mechanics of economic policy coordination; and (3) Community structural policies and finance. As regards coordination, three signs of movement in the Community should be noted. First, the Community is intensifying its three-times-a-year cycles of reviewing the economic situation and prospects, and it is considering the need for concerted policy moves. The "convergence decision" of February 18, 1974, provides the formal arrangements; and this fits with the timing of the European Council's meetings, which are increasingly concerned with the broad stance of economic policy. Second, in mid-1978 the Community prepared (in cooperation with the Bonn Western economic summit) a general shift in policy, with a Council decision in July 1978 detailing fiscal policy moves by each member state in a "concerted action program" aimed at improving growth in the second half of 1978 and in 1979. The beneficial effects of this action on the European economy have already been felt; however, the more general point is that experience was gained here of a new type of economic policy negotiation. Third, the EMS itself adds to the fabric of the coordination system through the consultations and action that will take place after the "divergence indicator" has been passed and through the prospective use of large amounts of conditional medium-term credit (see Jacques van Ypersele's paper).

The third category of action concerns the Community's own finances and policies. While the EMS's own technical characteristics required intense negotiation and compromise on several points, the issues that were resolved last lay outside the purely monetary domain. Three member states (Italy, the United Kingdom, and Ireland) claimed substantial budgetary resource transfers as part of the package, and France sought a stronger policy for reduction of agricultural monetary compensatory amounts (that is, the realignment of farm support prices, which at present vary between member states, with the aid of Community border taxes and subsidies).

The argument of the three "less prosperous" member states (as they were called in the text of the conclusions of the Bremen European Council of July 1978) were threefold. First, these countries were worried because the process of adjusting to the rigors of the EMS entailed a short-run risk of weakening the real economy. They also argued that, since economic and monetary union invariably contained a strong public finance redistribution function and since the EMS was meant to be a major step toward such union, the setting of the EMS should be accompanied by some significant parallel progress on the budgetary side. In addition, the United Kingdom's case was that the Community budget involved perverse, negative net transfers as far as it was concerned.

The outcome of the December European Council meeting was that the less prosperous countries fully joining the EMS (eventually Ireland and Italy) should receive, for each of five years, 200 million EUA of interest rate subsidies from the Community budget, matched with 1 billion EUA of Community loan finance from the Ortoli facility and the European Investment Bank, all the funds being devoted to financing infrastructure and investment projects. In addition, Ireland subsequently secured some further financial assistance bilaterally from certain other EMS participant countries.

Running parallel with the EMS negotiations were negotiations between the Council of Ministers, the Parliament, and the Commission on the size of the 1979 Community budget's allocation to the Regional Fund, which benefits predominantly the same three countries. The Council's first reading of the budget put 620 million EUA into the Regional Fund for 1979. The Parliament amended this up to 1,100 million EUA in October 1978, thus drawing attention to a number of important questions: political issues on the interpretation of the Parliament's budgetary powers, and financial issues concerning the scale of the Community's redistributive policies with or without the EMS. In a few words, by March 1979 the Council had adopted a revised 1979 budget, which, following new proposals by the Commission, incorporated the 200 million EUA of interest rate subsidies decided on at the European Council of December and a 945 million EUA Regional Fund.

Negotiations on Community finance also, however, had the effect of concentrating attention on the broader range of factors determining the relative economic performance of member states. There was little dissent from the view that the predominant factor should remain at the national level and that Community financial intervention could only be cast in a complementary role.

This complementary role has, however, two dimensions—in the structural policy function and the redistribution function—and it should be noted that the main instruments concerned (the Ortoli facility, the European Investment Bank, the Regional Fund, and the interest rate subsidies decided upon in the EMS negotiations) are addressed to both. The interaction of policy pressures can be illustrated with a number of examples. The continuing oil problem poses a threat to monetary stability. In the use of the new borrowing facilities energy projects are receiving high priority, and energy policy negotiations are heightened because of concern for the EMS. Countries that were the most uncertain about joining the EMS were the less prosperous areas, which are the main beneficiaries of regional policy instruments; Community regional policy has been strengthened because of the EMS. The monetary stability sought with the aid of the EMS has to go with better prospects for the real economy and thus offers the prospect of relief for acute sectoral problems such as those in steel and shipbuilding. Thus the Community's financial instruments are also aimed at the restructuring and reconversion of such sectors.

Last but not least the EMS is linked to the workings of the Common Agricultural Policy. One little-noticed effect has been to change the numéraire for farm prices from an old unit of account based on the working of the snake to the new EUA (or ECU). This particular technicality is not without importance. The numéraire now represents the full basket of Community currencies rather than a selection with a bias on the hard side.

This change marks the completion of several arduous years of reform of the Community's unit of account system, with unity now reestablished in the use of the single ECU for a hundred and one purposes ranging from the accounts of the Community's budget to the denomination of import duties that are defined in money amounts rather than percentages. As regards policy toward future accumulations of monetary compensatory amounts, the Agriculture Council in March moved a long way toward agreement that such amounts would be phased out within two years of their introduction. Overall the links between the EMS and agricultural policy have intensified the debate on the level of farm prices, the Commission having proposed a freeze for the 1979-80 farm price year.

Institutions

It will be evident that many Community institutions are involved in the EMS:

—the European Council, which makes strategic decisions;

—the Council of Ministers, which takes legislative action primarily in the Finance Council, but with related activity also in the Budget Council and the Agriculture Council;

—the Commission, which submits proposals for decision and is involved in general economic analysis and in the loan and budget financing;

—the Committee of Governors of Central Banks, especially when meeting as the Board of Governors of the European Monetary Cooperation Fund (EMCF);

—various committees of economic and monetary officials (Monetary Committee, Economic Policy Committee, alternates of Central Bank Governors);

—the European Investment Bank, which is involved in loan financing; and

—the European Parliament, which is involved in the political debate and in the budgetary legislation.

Coordination of these bodies is intricate, but on the whole the process of decisionmaking and negotiation has worked rapidly. It took exactly one year to get from the time the idea of the EMS was first discussed between heads of state and government to entry into operation in March 1979; and one and a half years from the time President Jenkins reactivated serious debate on European monetary integration in his October 1977 Florence lecture.

It is envisaged that within two years the EMCF will be consolidated in the establishment of a new European Monetary Fund. Work on this has hardly started. But the implications of the various possible means for transforming the EMCF (for which the Bank for International Settlements in Basel is at present the operating agent) into the precursor of a central monetary institution are clearly of primary importance.

Conclusion

The first major characteristic of the EMS is that it is a Community monetary system, deeply embedded in a whole range of Community institutions and their political, economic, and financial mechanisms. This was not true of the snake.

It is precisely because the EMS is intended to be a stride forward in the Community's general integration process that the special problems of Ireland, Italy, and the United Kingdom were accommodated in a tailor-made system. The core countries—Germany, France, Benelux, and Denmark, which are more interdependent, in part for reasons of closer proximity—were those for whom the advantages of monetary integration appeared most clear-cut. Ireland decided to join this "2¼ percent margin" group of core countries when it obtained assurance of quite substantial resource transfers to sustain its present rapid economic development. Italy wanted to join to help bolster its domestic stabilization efforts; it decided to do so with the aid of a more flexible 6 percent intervention margin and some resource transfers. For the United Kingdom the advantage was more difficult to assess. Eventually the decision was to participate in all features of the system except the intervention obligation, where the door remains open.

In the realm of macroeconomic policies the EMS is seen as reducing uncertainty, as providing a firmer monetary stability on which policy can be based. By 1977 countries prone to both devaluation and revaluation had come to appreciate that erratic exchange rate movements were part of the reason the European economy was being constrained to subpotential economic performance. Divergent exchange rates exacerbated divergent inflation rates, and this made it well-nigh impossible to control the European business cycle. The EMS aims at improving, at the margin, the real versus the price effects of the use of room for maneuver for expanding the European economy. These claims for the EMS are, of course, questions of judgment, and in theory a monetary union would handle the problems better than a fixed but adjustable exchange rate system. Since the Community is not yet ready to consider monetary union as an operational proposal, it has to proceed with more limited mechanisms. However, the EMS confirms the Community in its integrationist course and underlines the need to achieve convergence in economic performance. It is partly a long-run investment in institutional infrastructure. The payoff is in part to be expected only in the years ahead; it is certainly felt that the manageability of economic policy at the purely national level will continue to decline as economic interdependence increases.

Enlargement of the Community to include Greece, Spain, and Portugal will obviously not make the task of convergence easier. But the EMS is also a sign of political will to deepen as well as to enlarge the Community. Enlargement in these circumstances of course signals the political objectives of the Community. This illustrates the contrast between the snake and the EMS, even if technically there has been a smooth transition from one to the other; the former became a limited special purpose club, the latter aims to be central to the political structure of Europe.

Finally, the EMS is likely to aid work on many technically unrelated Community integration dossiers. It seems that there is a kind of symbiosis in Community affairs between the macro and the micro, the field of impersonal intergovernmental negotiations and the Europe of the citizen. If the Community's leaders show the will to do something important about the major macroeconomic problems, it increases the interest and the willingness of large numbers of officials, interest groups, and politicians to work away at the hundred and one Community dossiers that are less strategic in character but often closer to the lives of individuals.

Comments by Benjamin J. Cohen

Michael Emerson's paper, it seems to me, equates what the EMS is intended to be with what the EMS is likely to be. For example: "Will the EMS give a new boost to trade integration? The presumption and intention is yes." But to state an objective is not enough to assure its achievement. One must distinguish between the normative and the positive. The question is, given its intentions, can the EMS work?

Whether it works will depend on whether it can achieve convergence of economic policy and performance. Emerson, properly, stresses this requirement. Almost half his paper is devoted to the theme. He is also optimistic. The EMS will be "a strategic catalyst in the Community's political and economic integration," "a new spur to the Community integration process," and "confirms the Community in its integrationist course."

All of this sounds very much like the "monetarists" in the earlier debate on the European Monetary Union (EMU). Then, little wheels (exchange rates) were supposed to drive bigger wheels (economic policy and performance). It did not work in the EMU in 1972. Will it work now?

It certainly might work if exchange rates could be rigidly fixed. That would indeed be a "tonic for investors' confidence," "induce more migration," "attain both a lower average inflation rate and a lower dispersion of rates around this average," and "provide a firmer monetary stability on which policy can be based."

But exchange rates are not to be rigidly fixed. The EMS is to be a miniature Bretton Woods system—with fixed but adjustable exchange rates—and will therefore be subject to all the same difficulties as Bretton Woods. Given independence of national policies and capital mobility, speculative crises are inevitable. Present conditions are notably inauspicious for linking together the Community's currencies on any sustained basis. Inflation rates in Europe remain highly divergent, from a low of 3 percent in West Germany to more than 12 percent in Italy.

The new arrangement is consequently bound to be subjected to strain unless member states' policies can be coordinated more closely than heretofore. Chancellor Schmidt, however, has been obliged to promise a tight rein on credit transfers within the Community so as to placate domestic critics of the EMS (who have no wish to finance the anticipated inflationary excesses of others). Coordination in practice is thus likely to mean a deflationary bias toward Germany's inflation rate (as in the preexisting snake). This in turn will work to create unemployment problems that will cause grave tension within the EMS membership.[4]

For President Giscard d'Estaing, the potential for price discipline built into the joint float is actually one of its most attractive features, since this will complement his domestic commitment to firm anti-inflationary policies. For the Irish and the Italians, by contrast, the implied discipline of the EMS is more threatening. Herein lies the explanation for their insistence on larger transfers of resources through the European Investment Bank and, in Italy's case, on a broader band for movements of its currency. Similar fears account for Britain's initial decision to stay out altogether.

In one way or another, the new joint float will be liable to internal tensions. Either policy coordination will fail to reduce inflation differentials sufficiently or some of the weaker members will be unable to bear up under joint price discipline. In either case, strong centrifugal forces will be set in motion and speculators will have a field day. Member governments will then face a dilemma: either alter their exchange rates frequently or defend their linked rates with costly and ultimately futile intervention. Either course will undermine the stated goal of a "zone of monetary stability."

Doubts about the dollar would aggravate the EMS problem. Investors wishing to switch out of dollars are not attracted to weaker currencies like the lira or the French franc. They want strong currencies like the D-mark or the guilder (or yen or Swiss franc). Hence, renewed dollar sales would mean additional upward pressure on the stronger currencies relative to their weaker partners and even greater strain on the joint float.

4. It is not enough to say that this argument is based on a discredited Phillips curve. The Phillips curve does exist in the short run, which is the period that matters in real political life.

In the face of developing strain on the EMS, some participants may decide that the game is not worth the candle and withdraw from the arrangement. That is what happened to the EMU. There is little in the EMS design to suggest that history will not repeat itself.

It is instructive to ask why the Community's earlier EMU experiment failed. Originally, monetary unification had two motivations, one internal to the Community and one external. The internal motivation was to take another step on the road toward full economic and political union in Europe. The external motivation was to lessen dependence on the dollar and to enhance the Community's own monetary independence. It had long been evident that, lacking a common currency of their own, the European countries were obliged to rely on the dollar instead to achieve a kind of informal monetary integration. Since this also meant dependence on the monetary policy of the United States, it implied a partial loss of monetary sovereignty. Formal currency unification was viewed as the necessary condition for eliminating dollar hegemony. In addition, a common currency, which would undoubtedly become attractive to others for vehicle and reserve purposes, might also increase Europe's bargaining strength in international monetary discussions.

The experiment failed because member countries lacked the "political will" to make a common currency truly operational. At a lower level, national administrative hierarchies resisted all encroachments on their bureaucratic power and privileges. Central bankers, in particular, were unwilling to become submerged in a European "Federal Reserve System." And at a higher level, national political leaderships resisted all encroachments on their traditional decisionmaking authority. Governments were unwilling to transfer any significant portion of their formal policy sovereignty to Community institutions. Neither the internal nor the external motivation was sufficient to overcome these political obstacles. As a result, the dream of monetary unification lost all momentum. As the late Fred Hirsch wrote in 1972:

> In this sense one can conclude that European monetary integration is not a serious issue. It belongs to that category of commitments that are endorsed by national authorities at the highest level, but are in fact ranked low in their priorities when it comes to the test.[5]

So the questions remain. Can the EMS achieve convergence of economic policy and performance? Do the members have the political will now that was lacking in 1972?

5. Fred Hirsch, "The Politics of World Money," *The Economist* (August 5, 1972), p. 57.

In large measure, the answer depends on the Europeans themselves—specifically, on what is now most strongly motivating them to try again for monetary union. Greater monetary independence is manifestly one motivation. But monetary independence for what purpose? Are the Europeans trying to position themselves to share explicitly with the United States the responsibility for global monetary stabilization? Or are they simply trying to shield themselves as much as possible from a hegemonic leadership that they no longer regard as "responsible"? Put differently, are they animated by a sense of confidence in their relations with the United States or by a sense of distrust? Here is the real issue of the EMS for the United States.

An EMS motivated by a sense of mutual confidence would pose few difficulties for the United States. The problem, however, is that cooperation with the United States does not really seem to be what the Europeans have in mind. Much more crucial to their thinking is the distrust of American policy that has become so endemic in recent years, symbolized by the system's stated purpose to create a "zone of monetary stability" in Europe. The long decline of the dollar in 1977-78 wreaked havoc in European financial markets. The principal attraction of the EMS for most Community members is that it would help to shield them from similar instabilities in the future. Isolation from America, not cooperation, seems to be the main purpose of the exercise. And this clearly *will* pose difficulties for the United States.

In the first place, it means that even if the EMS were successfully implemented, it probably would not lead to a regime of shared responsibility for international monetary management. The Europeans are more likely to put some distance between themselves and the perceived threat of "malign" American nationalism, concentrating instead on the pursuit of their policy priorities mainly within the framework of their own regional Community. This certainly would not reduce the potential for policy conflict in global monetary relations. Nor would it reduce the danger of further pressure on the dollar through continued switching by investors into European currencies (or into the ECU, if and when it becomes available).

Worse, Europe's "isolationist" motivation suggests that the EMS may well never be successfully implemented. To succeed, the EMS must be a "serious issue." Preoccupation with outside instabilities is not enough. Governments must also demonstrate the political will to make the appropriate sacrifices of sovereignty—and this they have yet to do. Although they have once again endorsed the idea of monetary union at the highest political level, they still have not ranked it high among their practical policy priorities. In fact, they have all approached the project in a relentlessly self-interested manner, seizing the occasion to try to extract maximum national advantage for themselves. Community spirit has not been conspicuous.

The most probable outcome, therefore, is that the EMS, like its predecessor, will simply fail. Sooner or later, some weaker members will again be forced to abandon the joint float while the rest struggle on to preserve a truncated zone of stability around the D-mark. The Community's fragmentation will become even more pronounced, exchange markets will become even more unsettled, and the goal of shared responsibility for global monetary stabilization will become even more remote. For the United States, the outcome will probably be even greater pressure on the dollar.

This is admittedly a pessimistic projection, and it could be wrong. Perhaps European governments are now ready to make the sacrifices of sovereignty needed to make the EMS work. But experience and such evidence as we have seem to say that they are not.

Henri Baquiast

The European Monetary System and International Monetary Relations

My first proposition is that the European Monetary System is part of the process of integrating EC member countries' economies. It is one in a series of efforts and undertakings, all aimed at the gradual establishment of an economic and monetary union among the member countries of the European Community. The idea of a European monetary area goes back a long way. The need for monetary coordination became clear during the Common Market's infancy. Accordingly, in the absence of a single currency in the Community, it was decided to use units of account in many of its areas of activity, in particular the budget and common agricultural policy.

At the Hague Conference of the Heads of State and Government of the EC in December 1969, a decision was reached on the principle of achieving European monetary union step by step. In October 1970 the modalities of this union were the subject of a program prepared by a group of experts headed by Pierre Werner of Luxembourg. This program called for completion of monetary integration by 1980 and detailed the steps to be taken during an initial three-year period, notably the reduction of the fluctuation margins for European currencies and intervention in the exchange market in currencies of the Community.

Under the pressure of events that followed the August 1971 declaration of the inconvertibility of the dollar, the Werner plan as such proved infeasible. But early in 1972 the countries of the Community sought new responses in the monetary field to the situation created by the Smithsonian agreement of December 1971. These entailed in particular a broadening to ±2.25 percent of the maximum fluctuation of each currency in relation to its parity or central rate. By a resolution of March 21, 1972, the EC Council decided to reduce the fluctuation margin between European currencies to ±2.25 percent (from the 4.5 percent that prevailed under the independent links to the dollar) so that these currencies could be exchanged for each other under the

49

same terms as each of them could be exchanged for dollars. This was the snake in the tunnel decision.

In March 1973, following the decision to let the dollar float, the EC countries decided to maintain a joint float of their currencies (with the exception of the pound sterling and the Italian lira) independent of the dollar. The snake had come out of the tunnel. The European Monetary Cooperation Fund was established in June 1973, which made it possible to carry out intervention and settlement operations multilaterally.

New steps advancing monetary union were taken by the Commission in April 1974 when it submitted a proposal on the pooling of reserves within the Community. And in May 1975 French Minister of Finance Fourcade proposed a broadening of concerted efforts to determine a Community policy toward the dollar and other non-Community currencies. In February 1976 Minister of Finance Duisenberg of the Netherlands submitted a proposal for drawing European currencies together based on the idea of target zones. Finally, the interest in economic and monetary union shown in the Tindemans Report in 1976 should be mentioned.

The efforts toward monetary unification clearly have been numerous and persistent. Following this trend and taking into account past experience, the Heads of State and Government of the Community, meeting in Bremen in July 1978, decided to establish "a scheme for the creation of closer monetary cooperation leading to a zone of monetary stability in Europe," stressing that the scheme should be durable and effective.

The "Zone of Stability"

The basic objective of the EMS is both ambitious and simple: to create a zone of monetary stability in Europe. I should like to try to clarify the concept somewhat so as to avoid errors of interpretation.

First of all, the concept of a zone of stability does not mean that the countries of the Community intend to establish a kind of regional Bretton Woods system among themselves—that is, a geographically limited area within which a system of fixed parities, such as the one resulting from the initial Articles of Agreement of the International Monetary Fund, would continue to be applied. In reality, the EMS is clearly different from a regional Bretton Woods in both its principal characteristics and its objectives.

Its characteristics are more complex and more subtle. The EMS includes a number of new traits: the existence of wider margins, the possibility of adjusting the pivotal rates, the scope and flexibility of the different credit mechanisms, and last but not least, the creation of the ECU and its role in the system. All these arrangements clearly establish the originality of the new structure.

Moreover, the EMS can be distinguished from a regional Bretton Woods by its goals, which are more far-reaching than those of Bretton Woods and involve facilitating the economic integration of the member countries of the Community. By ensuring stable exchange rates between the currencies of the participating countries, the European Monetary System is pursuing three objectives:

—to stimulate the growth of trade within, and reinforce the cohesion of, the Community;

—to increase the effectiveness of policies in support of economic activities and promote more rapid growth;

—to gradually reduce the disparities between the rates of inflation in participating countries.

I will elaborate on these objectives.

First, a zone of monetary stability should reduce the distortions of trade within the Community that are attributable to speculative movements of exchange rates. Exchange crises and the excessive and sudden variations in exchange rates in recent years have had a negative effect on the functioning of the Common Market and on the export prospects of member countries. The ratio of trade within the Community to overall foreign trade of member countries is high. It currently represents 50 percent of sales and purchases for France and 56 percent for the EC countries as a whole. Adoption of the EMS will make it possible to shelter this portion of foreign trade from monetary disturbances and to stimulate its expansion.

Second, a zone of monetary stability should promote more rapid economic growth. Experience has shown that currency floating has had deflationary effects in the long run, both in countries with weak currencies and in those with strong currencies. In the weak-currency countries it has been observed that a decline in the exchange rate results in an immediate rise in the cost of essential imports such as energy and raw materials and thus contributes to an acceleration of the increase in the general level of prices. This in turn may result in a further drop in the exchange rate. There is thus the risk of entanglement in a cumulative process leading to a veritable "vicious circle." To escape such a result, the authorities must implement particularly harsh demand restriction policies, which curb growth.

Conversely, in countries whose currencies are tending to appreciate, an opposite "circle" phenomenon is taking place. Appreciation of the exchange rate gradually slows the expansion of exports and increases the uncertainty of business leaders about their future markets, prompting them to postpone new investments, again with the outcome of a slackening of growth.

Those EC countries experiencing difficult problems with unemployment need to sustain an adequate rate of growth of economic activity. The existence of stable exchange rates in the EMS should increase the effectiveness of national policies, promote economic activity, and make more rapid growth possible.

Third, the EMS should bring about a gradual reduction of the disparities between the inflation rates of participating countries. Here again, experience teaches that currency floating is accompanied by growing divergences between national inflation rates, which seriously threaten the prospects for European economic integration. The creation of a zone of monetary stability should contribute more effectively to slowing inflation by strengthening the self-discipline that its operating rules entail.

In sum, the concept of a zone of stability cannot be reduced to the notion of a regional zone of stable parities. It goes substantially further and becomes a fundamental effort to bring the several Community economies into convergence with one another.

The Indicator of Divergence

The effort to achieve such convergence is an essential element of the EMS. It will depend especially on a brand-new early warning device, the divergence indicator.

The divergence indicator is designed to detect Community currencies that happen to deviate upward or downward from the Community average as represented by the ECU. In practice, the difference between the daily rate in ECUs and the pivotal rate in ECUs is measured for each currency. A currency is not considered to diverge when this difference is below a certain threshold. The threshold for each currency is fixed at 75 percent of the maximum divergence spread between the rate in ECUs of the currency in question and its pivotal rate in ECUs. This maximum spread is reached when the currency reaches its intervention limit rate relative to all the other currencies. It is therefore different for each of the currencies and varies as a function of the relative weight of each currency in the ECU. The method of computation ensures that the appearance of the divergence signal will be independent of the relative weight of each currency in the ECU.

The divergence indicator will function on the presumption that, when a currency crosses its divergence threshold, the authorities of the country concerned will correct the situation by taking adequate measures; namely:

—diversified intervention (in particular by selection of appropriate intervention currencies);

—domestic monetary policy measures;

—changes in pivotal rates;

—other economic policy measures.

In case such measures are not taken because of special circumstances, the authorities of the country concerned must inform the other countries of the reasons, in particular when concerted action between central banks is taking place. Consultations will then take place in the appropriate Community bodies, including the Council of Ministers. This procedure should reinforce pressure for convergence. Much will depend, however, on the terms of its implementation. The main question is to find out whether the mechanism will or will not be binding in nature. Only experience will provide the answer.

There is also some question about the nature of the adjustment. Will it be symmetrical or will the burden be borne primarily by the weakest currencies? Here again, the results will depend on the manner in which the monetary authorities of countries with divergent currencies interpret the provisions relating to this mechanism. In any case, I believe, the indicator will result in action and will strengthen coordination of the economic policies of member countries.

The EMS and the International Monetary Fund

The EMS respects the objectives and the Articles of Agreement of the International Monetary Fund. Its operating rules are fully compatible with those of the IMF, whether for exchange arrangements and surveillance, for drawings on the Fund, for the role of lenders in the Fund, for the respective roles of the ECU and the special drawing right (SDR), or for payments and transfers.

As a zone of monetary stability, the new European system is compatible with the purposes of the IMF as defined in Article I of its Articles of Agreement, which include "to promote exchange stability, to maintain orderly exchange arrangements among members, and to avoid competitive exchange depreciation." The EMS is also compatible with the provisions of the amended Article IV of the Articles of Agreement, which expressly recognizes the possibility that the member countries of the IMF may adopt "cooperative arrangements by which members maintain the value of their currencies in relation to the value of the currency or currencies of other members" (Article IV, section 2[b]). In addition, the participating countries have, as required, notified the IMF of their participation in the new system upon its entry into force, and they will not fail to inform the IMF of any future changes in their exchange arrangements.

Finally, each participating country will be subject, like all member countries of the IMF, to the surveillance that the IMF shall exercise over exchange rate policies, in particular on the occasion of the annual consultations, but also in the course of the periodic discussions on the world economic outlook. The information required to that end will be communicated to the IMF by the European countries.

The new exchange rate system of the EC countries should therefore pose no more problems for the provisions of Article IV than did the snake system.

As for drawings on the IMF, no provision of the EMS imposes restrictions on drawings in accordance with Fund rules by participating EMS countries. The possibility that such drawings will occur depends on the size of the countries experiencing difficulties and on the extent and nature of the payments difficulties. But the existence of sizable Community credit mechanisms in no way means that recourse to the IMF by an EC country is excluded.

Furthermore, in the event that a country drew on the credit tranches and simultaneously had recourse to the medium-term financial assistance of the EMS, the terms of the two types of financial assistance could easily be brought into harmony. The recent example of Italy shows clearly that this need not present any difficulty. Italy concurrently used medium-term financial assistance from the EC and a standby agreement with the IMF. The conditions imposed by the two institutions were quite similar and certainly did not conflict. In both cases they dealt basically with the imposition of a ceiling on the money supply and credits to the economy and with reducing the public sector deficit and limiting treasury borrowing financed by the central bank. Similar coordination of conditionality is unlikely to present any problems in the future.

Contrary to a widespread notion, the IMF is not a worldwide central bank; drawings are purchases of foreign exchange financed by certain member countries, which thus become creditors of the Fund. These creditor countries ensure the liquidity of the IMF. In the past, some of the member countries of the EC whose payments positions were sufficiently strong have actively played the role of lenders of their own currency to the IMF. The fact that they belong to the EMS will not change this role. Accordingly, they are in no way induced to lose their interest in the functions and operations of the IMF even if recourse to the Fund by EMS members as borrowing countries may be less frequent henceforth.

The ECU is not in competition with the SDR. It is a reserve asset that can be held only by member countries. It will be usable only in making settlements between participants' central banks. As an asset it is strictly regional in nature and in use. Accordingly, it cannot compete with the SDR, which is held by 137 of the member countries of the IMF and by the IMF itself. Furthermore, the ECU was designed for this kind of regional use, since the basket of currencies making it up contains only the currencies of the member countries of the Community. It might further be stressed that the definition of the ECU is analogous to that of the European unit of account, whose existence had no negative effects on the SDR.

Finally, the European countries do not intend to give their regional liquidity needs (possibly to be met in part by the ECU) priority over the needs for liquidity of the world as a whole. In other words, the existence of the ECU will not make them lose sight of the need to examine world liquidity trends.

As for the existing structure of international transfers, it should be stressed that the EMS does not involve additions to existing exchange regulations. The EMS in no way entails the equivalent of a common exterior tariff. Its introduction does not call for special limitations on international capital movements.

Nor should the EMS affect the operating conditions of the international monetary system or outside currencies. It should first be recalled that intervention to limit fluctuations between European currencies is to be effected in principle in Community currencies, a practice that has no bearing on the currencies of nonmember countries. Experience with the functioning of the European monetary snake illustrates this lack of impact. On the contrary, it can be expected that third countries will profit from the advantages of greater monetary stability in Europe and that such stability may be favorable to stability in exchange relations with the other major currencies.

It is the attitude of the exchange market toward the relationships between the dollar (the major non-EC currency) and the other major national currencies, such as the yen and the Canadian dollar, that is important in determining the dollar's strength or weakness, rather than the fact that a group of European currencies are floating jointly. The exchange rate of the dollar is determined in relation to each of these other currencies. Its value therefore results from the weighted average of the various bilateral rates. But in the final analysis, what the market assesses and may sanction is the adequacy of the economic and monetary policy of the United States. It is therefore up to the United States to pursue the policies best suited for maintaining confidence in the dollar and ensuring the long-term stability of its currency.

Finally, the EMS will not change the real nature of the current international monetary system. The notion that the current system revolves around a single axis, the dollar, should not be accepted. No doubt that was the case in the period from 1945 to 1971, when the Bretton Woods agreements were in force, but that situation came to an end in 1973 with the floating of the major currencies. Moreover, if the exchange arrangements now in use by the other members of the International Monetary Fund are considered, it will be noted that several floating zones already exist: the dollar area, the SDR area, the European snake, the yen, the Swiss franc, and so forth. The abandonment of fixed exchange rates did not result in independent and individual floating on the part of all the member countries of the IMF. Rather, it resulted in the appearance of several zones, within which exchange relations are more or less organized or stabilized. In this respect, the introduction of the EMS does not change the nature of the existing international system. It involves no innovations and does not affect third currencies.

Conclusion

In the long term, it is certain that the EMS has a major potential for development. Among such potentialities, I shall mention only the prospects for the pooling of reserves, the issuance of a common currency, and the unification of domestic monetary policies. The European Monetary Fund, which will be established in two years, will probably be another step in this direction.

Future developments are hard to foresee. They will depend to a large extent on the results obtained from attempts at the convergence of national economies as well as on the more or less symmetrical nature of the policies adopted to promote it. Consequently, the future of the EMS should be assessed in terms of the progress made within the Community, not of abstract notions about the relationship of the EMS to the rest of the world.

Comments by Robert Solomon

Mr. Baquiast has given us a very clear paper on the EMS. Furthermore, I find it a reassuring paper since it responds in a constructive way to the major questions that have been raised about the impact of the EMS on the world economy and on the international monetary system.

Since there is very little of significance that I can find to disagree with in Baquiast's paper, I shall take up a few of the nuances in his presentation.

Baquiast goes to some lengths to refute the allegation that the EMS is simply a regional Bretton Woods system. I am quite willing to accept his characterization of the EMS. I also welcome his statement that protecting Europe against the vagaries of the dollar is not one of the purposes of the EMS.

One of the aspects of Baquiast's paper that particularly pleased me was his emphasis on the promotion of growth through the EMS. The rest of the world will certainly welcome the notion that the growth rate of Europe may be speeded up compared with its rate since the recession of 1975.

In his discussion of the zone of monetary stability in which more rapid growth will be promoted, Baquiast introduces the concept of the vicious circle and the virtuous circle in a system of floating exchange rates. He argues that in a floating rate system contractional effects are felt not only by countries with weak currencies but also by countries with strong currencies. I find this argument unconvincing. I believe that the sluggish performance of the so-called strong-currency countries in Europe in 1976-77 was a result of their domestic policies rather than of the appreciation of their exchange rates. In any event, we have to expect that exchange rate changes will take place from time to time in the EMS. Thus if there were a tendency to vicious and virtuous circles under floating, that tendency could also exist under an adjustable peg system. It is not evident, therefore, that the establishment of the EMS would eliminate the undesired effects of which Baquiast complains.

In this connection, I would like to mention a problem raised by the presentations of several of our friends from Europe. They seem to accept without question the notion that movements in relative prices provide a reliable guide to appropriate movements in exchange rates. In other words, they accept the purchasing power parity doctrine. My recent research and that of others throw grave doubt on the validity of this doctrine. To give one example, since early 1973 the effective exchange rate of the deutsche mark has increased almost 45 percent relative to the currencies of the other group of ten countries, but consumer prices in Germany relative to prices in the other ten countries have fallen only 19 percent. The purchasing power parity doctrine tells us that the D-mark is grossly overvalued. But no one believes this, given Germany's balance-of-payments position. Thus a more sophisticated guide to exchange rate adjustment will have to be developed in the EMS.

One can also raise a question about the statement that "currency floating is accompanied by growing divergences between national inflation rates."

Baquiast is careful not to say that the divergences are caused by floating. It is more plausible, in my view, to say that floating has continued because of the differences in inflation rates.

Baquiast goes on to tell us that the "zone of monetary stability should contribute more effectively to slowing inflation by strengthening the self-discipline" in the EMS. This is a bit vague and one would like to see a more extended discussion of just how a slowing of inflation will be brought about in the EMS countries with high inflation rates. We know that in none of them under current circumstances is the inflation a result of excess demand. Thus the nature of the discipline that would be imposed is not very clear. One can hope that it will be consistent with the growth objectives that Baquiast himself stresses when he describes the zone of monetary stability. In particular, one misses any mention of incomes policies in his paper.

In his discussion of the working of the divergence indicator, Baquiast raises two questions that are of considerable importance. One is, how will the operations of the divergence indicator influence the policies of member countries? That is, how constraining or binding will the divergence indicator be? He admits that only experience will answer this question. A second question has to do with the nature of the convergence. He asks whether it will be symmetrical or whether the burden will be borne by the weakest currencies, and once again the results will depend, he says, on how the monetary authorities interpret the divergence indicator. These are indeed important questions and it is refreshing to find that Baquiast has been frank enough to identify them.

There is little in Baquiast's discussion of the relationship of the EMS to the IMF and to the working of the monetary system that one can disagree with. He raises all the major questions one can ask about this relationship. Here and there he makes assertions without supporting them very strongly, but one can only be sympathetic with him. It is not possible to forecast precisely how the EMS will work in the future.

One could ask why it was necessary for the European countries to create a new reserve asset—the ECU—as a means of settlement. Why could they not have used the SDR for this purpose? Another question pertains to Baquiast's statement that the future value of the dollar depends in the final analysis on U.S. policies. This is true but incomplete. What happens to the dollar depends also on the policies of other countries. It takes two to tango.

Thus on the whole we are left without much to fear and even with increased optimism about Europe's future economic performance. Recent statements and actions in Europe, particularly in Germany, offer some reassurance to those who might have been concerned about the working of the EMS. It seems clear that the Bundesbank does not regard exchange rate stability as the most important objective of its policies. Presumably this will also be true of its feelings about the relationship of the deutsche mark to the currencies of the EMS. Thus Baquiast's optimism about the possibilities for growth in Europe seems justified, since imbalances among the EMS countries apparently are more likely to be dealt with by exchange rate realignments than by excessively restrictive monetary and fiscal policies in those countries that are in deficit.

Robert Triffin

The American Response
to the European Monetary System

A sensible response to the EMS requires, first of all, a determined attempt to "listen" before responding. I am very much concerned about American insularity, about our tendency to feel that we have the answers and that our only problem is to transmit our know-how to others who are less knowledgeable, less wise, less courageous, and less unselfish than we are.

Before summarizing my suggestions for an American response to the EMS, therefore, I shall, first, discuss the European motivations for taking such a step, in spite of the tremendous odds to be overcome, particularly the difficulties of reconciling national views and interests, of shaking the traditional inertia of bureaucracies, and of accepting the political—including the electoral—risks entailed in this bold attempt to reshape the future. And second, I shall outline a few crucial features of the EMS Agreement that seem to have escaped the attention of most official and academic observers in this country.[1]

Motivations

Why did the European Community belatedly agree to adopt a monetary system of its own rather than continue to rely on the Bretton Woods system—on a de facto or de jure U.S. dollar standard?

Note that it would have had to do so anyway, at some stage, as a first step toward the full economic and monetary union repeatedly promised over the past ten years by its heads of state and government. But why now? I shall skip the purely political motivations that contributed for so long to blocking an agreement and that have now, at long last, made it possible. Being an econ-

---

1. For a fuller discussion of the EMS, see John Williamson, Alexandre Lamfalussy, Niels Thygesen, and others, *EMS: The Emerging European Monetary System* (Ires, Louvain la Neuve, April 1979).

omist rather than a politician, I shall limit myself to a review of some of the economic arguments that explain this switch from a U.S. dollar standard to an EMS standard.

The Bretton Woods system enshrined the dollar as a "parallel currency" for Europe as well as for the rest of the world; that is, as a currency of denomination for most transnational contracts, a currency of settlement, of market intervention, and of reserve accumulation by central banks, a currency in which private firms and individuals accumulated most of their international working balances, and finally the currency against which national exchange rates were measured, stabilized, and "readjusted" by all countries other than the United States. This system worked with remarkable success until the end of the 1950s, gave evident and growing signs of its ultimate lack of viability in the 1960s, and finally broke down in the early 1970s.[2]

The EMS agreement reflects European dissatisfaction not with the Bretton Woods system itself, but with the actual functioning of the inconvertible paper-dollar standard that took its place eight years ago and with the generalized, nationally managed, floating rate system that has been used to palliate some of the defects of this paper-dollar standard in the past six years. Speaking of Europe only—ignoring the views of the members of OPEC, of the other less developed and developed countries, and of the communist countries—I shall mention three major reasons for this dissatisfaction and for the Community's attempt to establish a different system.

The first is the inflationary flooding of the international monetary system by an unrestrained dollar creation. I shall mention only two broad developments as evidence of what we all know. The foreign exchange reserves (overwhelmingly dollars) of European central banks have grown tenfold since 1969 (from less than $13 billion to more than $133 billion at the end of 1978), increasing over these nine years by nine times as much as in all previous years and centuries since Adam and Eve. The inflationary implications of such a reserve explosion are obvious, since it entailed for the European central banks a $120 billion increase in their "high-powered money" issues, multiplied further by commercial banks under the traditional system of fractional reserve requirements, legal or customary. The parallel explosion in the foreign loans of the European commercial banks must also be noted. Those recorded by

2. I apologize for mentioning my early warnings of this impending breakdown, particularly in my testimony to the Joint Economic Committee of Congress in October 1959. The official collapse of the system began with the so-called two-tier gold price hurriedly adopted in March 1968, and was consummated by the "temporary" suspension of dollar convertibility in August 1971 and the generalization of floating exchange rates in March 1973. See the article by John Williamson in *EMS*.

the Bank for International Settlements (BIS) amounted to nearly $500 billion in mid-1978; $92 billion of this was in domestic currencies and $400 billion in foreign "Eurocurrencies," of which $276 billion was in Eurodollars.

A second reason for the Europeans' growing dissatisfaction was the huge losses entailed by their accumulation of depreciating dollars. In real purchasing power, the dollar has declined by more than half over the past ten years (by more than 50 percent if measured by the rise of wholesale prices, and by about 60 percent if measured by the rise in the unit value of exports).

More relevant as a measure—considering conceivable alternatives to dollar accumulation of liquid reserves and working balances—is the depreciation of the dollar in relation to other currencies. The so-called effective exchange rate of the dollar vis-à-vis twenty major currencies (as measured by the International Monetary Fund and published monthly in *International Financial Statistics*) had declined in December 1978 by 24 percent since May 1970. While highly relevant in other respects, this measure is totally irrelevant as a guidepost for reluctant dollar holders, since a moderate decline was heavily influenced by the rise of the dollar relative to the Canadian dollar, the pound sterling, the Mexican peso, and so forth.

The practical alternatives for holders of U.S. dollars are not these weak currencies but the stronger currencies, particularly the Japanese yen, the German mark, and the Swiss franc, which had risen in the same period by 83 percent, 95 percent, and 161 percent, respectively, in relation to the dollar, entailing a dollar depreciation of 45 percent, 49 percent, and 61 percent vis-à-vis these currencies. These huge fluctuations were undoubtedly due in large part to capital movements by Americans as well as by foreigners. They may be "blamed" on "speculators," but in a free enterprise economy the private sectors are expected to be guided by the profit motive, and daily floating rates are expected to induce corporation treasurers and others to switch promptly from depreciating to appreciating currencies. The task of stabilizing the dollar, or at least avoiding unnecessary, excessive fluctuations, devolves not on them but on the public authorities.

As far as central banks are concerned, the use of the dollar as the main component of international reserve accumulation entailed enormous bookkeeping losses. Those reported by the Bundesbank, for example, totaled 43 billion deutsche marks in an eight-year period (1971-78). At the December 31, 1978, dollar-mark exchange rate (1.828 marks per dollar) this would translate into a $23.6 billion loss, more than three times the total international reserves of Germany at the end of 1969.

Third, even if full confidence in the dollar were restored tomorrow, the desire for a different system less utterly dependent on it would still be explainable so long as responsible policymakers did not base their decisions on the unrealistic assumption that Americans—any more than they—could be relied on to have permanent wisdom, courage, and luck in "keeping their house in order" indefinitely.

In any case, the short- and medium-term prospects for the dollar are not all that bright under the present international monetary system, or "nonsystem." Table 1 shows a growing annual increase in the foreign indebtedness incurred by the U.S. Treasury and commercial banks—excluding their branches abroad—from $2 billion in 1970 to $10 billion in 1975, $32 billion in 1976, $44 billion in 1977, and $53 billion in 1978 (line I-A). If other foreign holdings (such as direct and portfolio investments) and errors and omissions are included, total indebtedness abroad (line III) rose in 1978 by $75 billion, that is, by more than the gross international monetary reserves of the rest of the world at the end of 1969 ($61 billion). Of the $75 billion, only 17 percent ($13 billion) financed the U.S. deficit on current account (line III-A); 83 percent ($62 billion) financed the "recycling" of foreign surpluses and deficits through American capital exports (line III-B). When these estimates for 1975-78 are added up, the international role of the dollar as a "recycling" currency overexplains the $198 billion cumulative increase in foreign indebtedness: capital exports amounted to $195 billion and the current account showed a small surplus of $2 billion.

This is not to say, however, that the current account transactions of the United States have been satisfactory from a normative policy point of view. Economically as well as humanly, one of the richest and most capitalized countries in the world should find it both possible and desirable to contribute at least 1 percent of GNP to the financing of the poorer and less capitalized countries. Last year this goal, which has been piously proclaimed in many United Nations resolutions, would have entailed *real* capital exports—a current account *surplus*—of about $21 billion, instead of a deficit of $13 billion (or $33 billion if net earnings on past investments are excluded from the current account balance). The gap to be corrected may thus be estimated at $34 billion or $54 billion a year, depending on whether or not earnings on *past* investments are regarded as a *current* contribution to foreign countries' development.

Fourth, widespread doubts about the future exchange rates of the dollar are based not only on speculative forecasts of the current account balance, but also on the danger of capital switches from the dollar "overhang" accumulated as a result of past deficits into other currencies or assets abroad. I have

Table 1. Balance of Payments of the United States[a]

Billions of dollars

Item	1970	1975	1976	1977	1978[b]
I. Increase in indebtedness (−)	−8	−15	−37	−51	−63
A. Of Treasury and banks to:	−2	−10	−32	−44	−53
1. Official authorities	−8	−7	−18	−37	−34
2. Private sector (mostly banks)	6	−3	−14	−7	−19
B. Other	−6	−5	−5	−6	−10
II. Errors and omissions	...	−5	−9	1	−11
III. Total financing	−8	−22	−46	−50	−75
A. Current U.S. deficits (−)	4	21	7	−13	−13
1. Net earnings on past investments	6	13	16	18	20
2. Merchandise balance	3	9	−9	−31	−34
3. Other	−5	−1	1	1	1
B. Capital exports ("recycling") (−)	−11	−43	−53	−37	−62
1. Monetary reserves	3	−1	−3	...	1
2. Banks	−1	−14	−21	−11	−34
3. Foreign aid	−3	−6	−7	−6	−8
4. Other	−9	−22	−22	−19	−21
Addendum:					
Average dollar depreciation (−) or appreciation (+) since May 1970 (in percent) relative to:					
20 major currencies	...	−16	−12	−13	−21(−24)
Swiss franc	...	−41	−43	−45	−59(−62)
German mark	...	−33	−31	−37	−45(−49)
Japanese yen	...	−18	−18	−26	−42(−45)
British pound	...	+8	+33	+38	+25 (+21)

Sources: Balance-of-payments estimates, *Survey of Current Business*, various issues; exchange rates, *International Financial Statistics*, various issues, United States page, lines *a m x* for the weighted average ("effective rate") of the dollar vis-à-vis twenty major currencies, and *a h x* for its bilateral rates vis-à-vis the Swiss franc, the deutsche mark, the yen, and the pound.

a. This presentation is designed to highlight the impact of the international role of the dollar as a "parallel currency":

(1) the yearly piling up of direct U.S. indebtedness abroad (line 1), and particularly that of the U.S. Treasury and commercial banks (line I-A), excluding their foreign branches;

(2) the contribution of these borrowings—willful or unwillful—including "errors and omissions" to the financing of (a) the deficits on current account—excluding government grants—of the *United States* (line III-A); and (b) the "recycling" by the United States of *other countries'* deficits (line III-B), and particularly the capital exports of U.S. banks' head offices; and

(3) the depreciation of the dollar vis-à-vis other major currencies in spite of this financing.

b. Figures in parentheses are average dollar depreciation or appreciation as of December 1978.

not yet calculated the latest estimates derivable from the *Federal Reserve Bulletin* and the *Survey of Current Business,* but the addition of the 1978 deficits to the overhang at the end of last year—uncorrected for huge valuation adjustments and particularly exchange rate adjustments—would show a stock indebtedness of more than $260 billion for the U.S. Treasury and the head offices of American banks, *plus* close to $170 billion of liabilities to foreigners of the overseas branches of U.S. banks. The total of about $430 billion should be compared with $78 billion at the end of 1969. It does not include other Eurodollar liabilities created by foreign rather than U.S. banks. The total dollar and Eurodollar liabilities of U.S. banks ($89 billion) and their offshore branches ($101 billion) and of European banks including U.S. branches ($299 billion) last September totaled $489 billion, plus, undoubtedly, a portion of the $57 billion liabilities of Canadian and Japanese banks.[3]

Last but not least, the Europeans are deeply concerned about the impact that a further depreciation of an already vastly undervalued, overcompetitive dollar rate would have on their own economic activity and employment in the sectors competing abroad and at home with U.S. exports. The estimates of *International Financial Statistics* show, for instance, that U.S. competitiveness in manufacturing improved from 1970 to the third quarter of 1978, in relation to Germany, by about 16 percent in export unit values, 39 percent in terms of value added deflators, and 47 percent in terms of normalized unit labor costs.

Features of the EMS Insufficiently Understood in the United States

I leave it to others to review the main features of the new EMS and of its prospective evolution in the forthcoming months and years. All I wish to do

3. These estimates are derived from the latest BIS quarterly report, and are not fully comparable with those of the *Federal Reserve Bulletin.* The BIS report regards as "foreign" the liabilities of non-U.S. banks to U.S. residents but not those to residents of the host country, while the *Federal Reserve Bulletin* estimates include as foreign liabilities of U.S. branches those to residents of the host country but exclude those to U.S. residents. For comparison's sake, the gross size of the Eurocurrency market was estimated in the March 1979 issue of *World Financial Markets* as being $795 billion at the end of September 1978 (the BIS estimate was $764 billion) and $860 billion at the end of December, of which about 73 percent was in Eurodollars at the end of September ($580 billion then, and $628 billion at the end of the year, if the percentage of Eurodollars remained the same).

is dispel a few widespread misunderstandings still entertained in this country by many economists, in official and particularly in academic circles.

Even those most in favor of European monetary and political union remain basically skeptical about its success, and indifferent or even downright opposed to it. This is to be expected, of course, from those who are enthusiastic about free markets and floating exchange rates. I shall not enter again this unending debate.

I can agree, on the other hand, with those who hold that commitments to exchange rate stability would be premature, harmful, and bound to fail as long as member countries have not succeeded in reducing the wide divergences still prevailing in their national rates of inflation (although these are in part the result, as well as the cause, of divergent fluctuations in exchange rates). This view is widely shared by the promoters of the EMS and indeed has inspired some features, noted below, designed to accelerate rather than prevent the exchange rate readjustments still expected to be inevitable in the early years of the system. Full monetary union and irrevocable exchange rate stability remain distant hopes, not thought to be achievable at this stage. The initial phase of the EMS centers—like the most successful monetary agreement ever concluded, the European Payments Union—on immediately feasible goals and acceptable commitments, rather than on blueprints for the distant future. Even the most chauvinistic opponents of full-fledged monetary union can agree on it insofar as it aims to promote the use of the ECU as an alternative to widely used foreign currencies and Eurocurrencies, including Eurodollars, in international payments.

Let me merely mention seven crucial features of the system that are highly attractive to its promoters.

In the first place, the system restores for the participating currencies a common denominator—or numéraire—sadly lacking in the revised IMF Articles of Agreement. In the absence of such an agreed-upon common denominator the dollar was the only common denominator used by the exchange market, and until recently tended to be the point of reference used by the authorities in calculating exchange rates and their readjustments. Perfectly logical under the Bretton Woods system, this procedure became absurd after the dollar became inconvertible and other currencies were left to fluctuate widely relative to each other and to the dollar. More and more countries thus began to calculate "effective" exchange rates in relation to national "baskets" of the currencies of the countries most important in their external transactions.

The U.S. dollar is not a major component of such baskets for any country of the Community. It may be gauged from table 1 of Michael Emerson's paper that the United States absorbs an average of less than 6 percent of the Community countries' exports, this percentage ranging in 1976 from a low of less than 3 percent for the Netherlands to a high of 9.6 percent for the United Kingdom. Intra-Community exports account, on the average, for 52 percent of the exports of participating countries, with a range of 36 percent to 77 percent for individual countries. The addition of services, such as tourism, transportation, and insurance, to merchandise exports would probably raise these percentages substantially as far as current account transactions are concerned.

Moreover, most other countries of Western Europe—to say nothing of Eastern Europe, Africa, and the Middle East—are likely to associate themselves de facto or even de jure with the EMS. Adding to the intra-Community trade only the Community's exports to other European OECD countries brings the average share of exports covered by the EMS arrangements to 67 percent—twelve times the Community's exports to the United States—ranging from a low of 51 percent for the United Kingdom's exports to a high of 92 percent for the exports of the Belgium-Luxembourg Economic Union.

All in all, the member countries of the Community and others closely associated with it in their external transactions are likely to account for three-fourths or even more of the Community's current transactions on trade account. The adoption of the ECU as a common denominator for exchange rate quotations, stabilization, and readjustments therefore appears to be a highly reasonable objective.

Second, the adoption of a "divergence indicator," which places on the country with the divergent currency the presumptive burden for the readjustment of domestic policies or exchange rates, or both, should help accelerate desirable readjustments. In contrast to the IMF Articles of Agreement as well as to the "snake" agreement, consultations on such readjustments are no longer left exclusively to the initiative of the country in question. The process can be triggered as well by partner countries complaining of the impact of an undervalued or overvalued exchange rate on their own economies. This is an unprecedented breakthrough in international monetary arrangements.

Third, Article 107 of the Rome Treaty requires that "each Member State handle its policy regarding exchange rates as a problem of common interest." The adoption of the ECU as common denominator gives, for the first time, an operational significance to this provision. I refer you to the March 1979 *Bundesbank Bulletin* for a full explanation of this matter, and quote only the following sentences from the relevant passage (page 13):

> It follows from the choice of the ECU as the fixed numéraire for the central rates of participating countries that a change in the ECU central rate of one

currency necessarily leads to changes in the ECU central rates of other currencies. . . . Any change in a central rate in the EMS is therefore carried out in the context of a realignment of all ECU central rates, and it is consequently subject to the agreement of all the participants in the system.

Fourth, and particularly important to the United States, will be the replacement—in principle, at least—of the dollar by Community currencies in market interventions and by the ECU in the settlement of mutual credits. Americans have often justifiably complained of the dominant use of the dollar for both of these purposes, as strong—even though unintended—upward or downward pressure could be exerted on the market rates of the dollar, irrespective of any development in the underlying balance of payments of the United States, whenever Community countries' surpluses or deficits switched from eager to reluctant dollar holders, or vice versa. For instance, the dollar's strength in the exchange markets in 1977 was largely due to the accumulation by the United Kingdom and Italy of $17.5 billion of foreign exchange in 1977 (more than doubling Italy's depleted foreign exchange reserves and septupling those of the United Kingdom). Its precipitous decline in 1978 got much of its impetus because the United Kingdom had to sell dollars to finance its deficit, adding to the dollars that more reluctant dollar holders, such as Germany, Switzerland, and Japan, had to add to their already bloated holdings in order to slow the excessive appreciation of their currencies on the market.

The European motivation for a switch to ECU settlements is different, however. Central bankers have finally come to realize that repayment provisions and even terminology have been outmoded by the inconvertibility and huge fluctuations of the dollar. A concrete example illustrates this point more vividly than any abstract argument. For instance, the National Bank of Belgium was occasionally required, under the snake agreement, to buy German marks when the mark reached its bilateral floor against the Belgian franc on the exchange market. This was dubbed a "loan" to the Bundesbank and called for quick repayment. The Bundesbank would "repay" the loan a few weeks later by taking back its marks and giving the National Bank in exchange unguaranteed dollars, which fluctuated sharply downward during the following months. Why should a claim on a member country of the Community be called a loan, and its replacement by an unguaranteed claim on a nonmember country (the United States) be called a repayment?

The substitution of the ECU for the dollar in such settlements might, of course, reduce the United States' deficit-financing facilities. Unpleasant as this would be in the short run, it might nevertheless be deemed beneficial in the longer run because it would restore a balance-of-payments and monetary discipline whose excessive relaxation has undoubtedly contributed for a long time to policies leading to a disastrous overvaluation of the dollar abroad and an inflationary weakening of its purchasing power at home.

One of the German motivations for the EMS is the hope that it may direct to other European currencies and to the ECU itself some of the speculative flows from weaker currencies into the deutsche mark. Germany, like Switzerland, complains bitterly about the excessive appreciation of its currency caused by the "refuge currency" status forced upon it by speculators. The first months of functioning of the EMS have indeed been encouraging in this respect (though in part for extraneous reasons, upon which I cannot dwell here). Weak currencies, such as the lira, the Irish pound, and the Danish krone have moved up well beyond their central rates while the D-mark has hovered around, mostly below, its central rate. The spreading of the previous "refuge currency" role of the strong currencies would, of course, be helpful to the dollar also by reducing its excessive bilateral depreciation relative to these currencies, often taken by speculators as a signal to unload more dollars on the market.

Fifth, the ECU is too often described by uninformed writers as a mere unit of account. The previous paragraphs—and the EMS Agreement—have already emphasized its roles as numéraire and as a means of payment and reserve accumulation by central banks. Its official use is spreading daily to many other Community transactions. It is also likely to be used in the near future as an alternative to Eurodollars, Euromarks, and so forth, in the flotation of bond obligations by the Community, the European Investment Bank, and even by national and local authorities. Equally important is the prospect that commercial banks may offer their customers ECU-denominated loans and deposits as an alternative to the Eurocurrency denominations prevalent today. Actual and prospective developments in this respect were summarized in my December 1978 *Foreign Affairs* article and need not be rehashed here.

For a sixth point—and for brevity's sake—I merely refer to the same article for a discussion of the transition to full monetary union and the merger of national currencies, when and if EMS succeeds in attaining its ultimate objective of stability in intra-Community exchange rates.

Finally, let me mention that a full-fledged commitment to monetary union would require more than even a prolonged de facto stabilization of exchange rates. It would require a transfer of jurisdiction from national authorities—and their advisers—to Community institutions. The proposed European Monetary Fund would pave the way for such an evolution, modestly initiated already by the transfer to the European Monetary Cooperation Fund (EMCF) against ECU balances of 20 percent of each country's gold and dollar reserves. This percentage could be increased in time to encompass, not a pooling, as it is often improperly described, but joint management by their holders of international reserves now entrusted largely to the management of the U.S. monetary authorities and commercial banks.

Suggestions for the U.S. Response

I now come to my personal suggestions for an American response to the EMS. First, I should say that I strongly favor a positive and constructive response, in a spirit of cooperation rather than one of skepticism, indifference, fear, or latent opposition.

The EMS should be viewed as an unprecedented opportunity to help the United States and the world resolve the awesome dollar problem, which is the legacy of the ill-advised and ill-fated dollar exchange standard of yesteryear. It might also, in a longer perspective, guide us toward a renewed, imperatively required effort to shape a worldwide monetary system worthy of its name and fair and acceptable to all concerned, including the less developed and the communist countries.

Europeans share with Americans a deep desire to restore the dollar as a currency worthy of the richest and most powerful country in the world. As stressed in the first part of this paper, a further weakening of the dollar exchange rates to even more undervalued, overcompetitive levels than is already the case would be as unacceptable to them as to us. It could hardly fail to trigger protectionist restrictions abroad against what would be called "exchange-rate dumping," followed by panicky moves here toward similar restrictions and even toward exchange controls that would be particularly disastrous for a world reserve center and a parallel currency.

The first requirement will be the correction of the huge and growing deficits of recent years, and indeed the restoration of healthy surpluses in the U.S. balance of payments on current account. This, in turn, will require an even more determined fight to reduce oil consumption and imports and a rate of domestic inflation that is double or triple that of Germany, Japan, Belgium, the Netherlands, or Austria, to say nothing of Switzerland. The clear affirmation of these prior policy objectives by the Congress and the administration, and their early implementation by concrete restraints on fiscal overspending, excessive money creation, price and wage increases, oil consumption and imports, and so on, should help restore confidence in the dollar and reverse bearish speculation against it by Americans and by foreigners. The measures announced and put into operation since last November have already shown substantial results.

Still, a total and lasting correction of external deficits cannot be expected overnight. Corrective policies—including past readjustments of exchange rates—produce their effects slowly. Avoiding an excessive depreciation of the dollar will still require considerable financing of foreign deficits for some time to come.

The United States can draw for this purpose on its own international reserves, which were estimated at $21 billion at the end of January 1979 but which would actually approximate $75 billion if gold holdings were revalued at the current market price of gold. This latter estimate is, of course, excessive, since gold prices would collapse in the event of massive sales. It is relevant, however, as one of the many reassurances to prospective creditors about the United States' solvency.

Far more important is the willingness, amply demonstrated already, of foreign countries to participate in a joint defense of agreed-upon dollar rates. This would include the adjustments, upward as well as downward, that might be deemed appropriate—or unavoidable—before any stabilization of the dollar in relation to the other major currencies could be realistically envisaged, even as a presumptive goal rather than as a legally binding commitment. The radical policy changes announced on November 1, 1978, are essential in this respect.

The U.S. government has agreed to intervene heavily in the exchange market rather than leave such interventions nearly exclusively to others. It has agreed to reduce the inflationary impact of borrowing abroad by borrowing in the financial market rather than nearly exclusively from central banks. The United States is now ready to denominate foreign borrowing in the creditors' currencies as well as in dollars in order to make them more attractive and acceptable to prospective lenders deterred by the risk of exchange losses on a depreciating dollar. It is now willing to explore with its IMF partners the opening of so-called substitution accounts in SDRs as a way to mop up some of the dollar overhang accumulated in the past.[4]

The EMS opens up new opportunities in all of these respects.

The adoption of the ECU as a parallel currency may soon enable the United States to denominate some official foreign borrowings in ECUs. Financially, this would expose the United States to smaller risks of exchange losses than

---

4. Agreement on this technique, however, is likely to require a parallel agreement of some sort on the complementary proposal of the IMF executive directors and the Committee of Twenty on "asset settlements."

alternative denominations in national currencies such as the mark or the Swiss franc. Politically, it would be a concrete and spectacular demonstration of the will to support the new European Monetary System. And it would be far more acceptable than borrowing in any national currency other than the dollar, borrowing that would open the way to charges that the dollar was becoming a satellite of, say, the mark.

A reinforced EMCF—and later a European Monetary Fund—should facilitate joint interventions and management of European exchange rates vis-à-vis the dollar. It should also provide an additional mechanism for substitution accounts. Reluctant dollar holders could exchange them for ECUs if they wished, as well as for SDRs.

The quid pro quo of the exchange guarantees granted by the United States to the EMCF would be a substantial lowering of interest rates on its obligations, and their consolidation into longer-term maturities. This consolidation vis-à-vis the EMCF would leave intact the "liquid" character of the ECU claims held on it by the national central banks in exchange for their dollars, insofar as the intra-EMS balance-of-payments disequilibria could be settled by mere bookkeeping transfers of ECU balances from one member country to another. This liquid character would also be preserved for the financing of European deficits with the United States—and other dollar-area countries—if U.S. obligations to the EMCF were expressed in the most appropriate form, that is, in "consols" without any imperative repayment date. Consol bonds paying interest to their holders but repayable only at the initiative of the debtor—mostly through open market operations—used to be a traditional and prestigious means of borrowing for the British government, and under the name of "rentes perpétuelles," for the French government. They could be made similarly familiar and attractive today, especially if coupled with a "contingent" repayment obligation in the event that balance-of-payments disequilibria were reversed and present creditors were again to incur substantial deficits with the United States. This would, moreover, express operationally an inescapable truth: that "real" repayment of international credits can only be effected through the recovery of a surplus position by the debtor. All that financial arrangements can do otherwise is to reshuffle among the creditors the claims on a deficit country. Similarly, these creditors can only receive "real" repayment for their claims by running deficits. I believe that adopting the suggestions above would help to dispel the financial fog obscuring these transactions —which often misleads the transactors themselves into unfortunate and ineffective policy decisions—and adjust international lending practices to the facts of life.

I shall comment only briefly on suggestions relating to the insertion of the EMS and the EMS-U.S. agreements into the broader framework of world monetary reform. I hope I am not entirely alone in feeling that floating rates and the second amendment to the IMF Articles of Agreement should not relegate to the trash can all the previous proposals for IMF reform, which were worked out during ten years of continuous, intensive negotiations. I refer those of you who are still open to argument on this score to my inaugural McCloy lecture of November 1978 published by Princeton University in *Essays in International Finance* under the title "Gold and the Dollar Crisis: Yesterday and Tomorrow" (particularly pages 11 and 12). The revolutionary developments of recent years certainly require a modification of previous proposals for reform. But the need is to enlarge them—particularly to deal with the fantastic explosion of private international credits—rather than to emasculate them.

I consider that a successful functioning of the EMS and of the links to be established between it and the dollar area may provide invaluable guidelines for the reforms that will be negotiable and feasible on a global scale. A decentralized IMF system should leave to regional organizations such as the EMS wide responsibilities and initiatives for the handling of problems between their members, and reserve for the IMF only the problems that cannot be dealt with as, or more, efficiently on a regional scale. This should elicit from like-minded countries that are interdependent and sufficiently aware of this interdependence closer cooperation—even integration—than is feasible in a broader framework between more heterogeneous groups of countries. It should also make it possible to reintegrate into the international monetary community the countries—especially the communist countries—to which a needlessly centralized Bretton Woods system anchored to the national currency of a single superpower was obviously unacceptable.

Comments by Ralph C. Bryant

I am broadly in agreement with Robert Triffin's statement and, subject to some exceptions, which I will note, with his specific conclusions as well. Rather than focus on points about which we differ, it seems more useful to take up the important general issues he raised and, in so doing, supplement his remarks.

First, Triffin is surely right in saying that the attitude of the United States toward the EMS should be to listen and learn. Nothing can be lost by a response that is positive and constructive. It is hardly the part of Americans or American authorities to condemn or dismiss out of hand an initiative that has the blessing of the senior political leaders of the European Community and on which rest some of the hopes for the Community's future.

Saying this does not rule out skepticism about the EMS design. Nor, for that matter, does it exclude worry about the possible implications of the EMS for the IMF and for the world as a whole. An American can offer this qualification since the United States has had a less than distinguished record of concern for the IMF and occasionally for the global economy. There are reasons to worry, not just about how Europe may behave, but also about possible North American responses

Triffin advances a comforting thesis involving two levels of monetary cooperation, regional and global, which he sees as complementary rather than competitive. The Community nations will act together within the EMS and also contribute fully to the operations of the IMF. I agree with Triffin that the two levels can and should be complementary; this is roughly analogous to the proposition that in domestic affairs different levels of government can provide different sorts of public goods, to the general benefit.

But each nation's government has limited capacities for cooperation with other governments. Conceivably, although not probably, most of the European energy for supranational consultation and cooperation could go into European institutions like the EMS and into European-North American-Japanese relations. Similarly, the United States might, by inadvertence as much as by design, give too much attention to problems related to a stronger and unifying Europe at the expense of wider or global considerations. The IMF and cooperation at the world level might be the losers by omission rather than commission.

In 1973, I remember, a cynical comment made the rounds of the IMF's Committee of Twenty: "When a small country and the IMF disagree, the small country gets in line; when a large country and the IMF disagree, the IMF gets in line; when the large countries disagree among themselves, the IMF disappears."

The IMF has not disappeared, of course. But we should keep reminding ourselves of the need for a strong, vigorous IMF. Like it or not, the monetary problems of the future will not be confined within regional bounds. The requirement for cooperative actions on a global scale will continue and grow. All of us would lose if the Community and the United States were to allow themselves to be diverted from this reality.

Let me turn now to a second broad issue, the question of exchange rate variability. Conventional wisdom in international economics argues that floating rates insulate national economies from one another. To quote from Milton Friedman's classic essay: "Flexible exchange rates are a means of combining interdependence among countries through trade with a maximum of internal monetary independence" and "are a means of permitting each country to seek for monetary stability according to its own lights, without either imposing its mistakes on its neighbors or having their mistakes imposed on it.[5]

A sound macroeconomic analysis of open economies allowing for financial as well as real-sector interdependence undermines this conventional view just as it undermines the untrammeled-market position about exchange rate variability.[6] Under conditions of intermediate interdependence there is *no* way to achieve insulation from economic and financial developments in other nations. Monetary policy actions taken in foreign countries affect both financial and real-sector variables in the home economy, whatever happens to the exchange rate. Monetary policy actions by the home country central bank cannot be bottled up at home, regardless of the manner and degree of exchange rate flexibility. Analogous conclusions apply to the international consequences of nonpolicy disturbances.

To illustrate, consider for a moment a world of two nations, America and Europe. Suppose the central bank of America engages in an expansionary "domestic" open market operation (that is, buys dollar-denominated securities and thus expands the domestic monetary base), and consider the effects of that action on Europe. The action puts incipient pressure on the dollar to depreciate in the exchange market (an appreciation of the European currency). If the central bank intervenes in the exchange market to keep the exchange rate unchanged and if the European central bank holds interest rates in Europe steady, the external reserves and monetary base of Europe rise. If the exchange rate is kept stable and the European central bank keeps the monetary base in Europe unchanged, external reserves and domestic interest rates in Europe rise. If the European currency is allowed to appreciate while the European central bank keeps interest rates in Europe unchanged, the European monetary base is altered. If the European currency appreciates and the monetary base in Europe is held stable, European interest rates are altered. In no conceivable case can all key financial variables in Europe remain unchanged after

5. *Essays in Positive Economics* (University of Chicago Press, 1953), p. 200.

6. These comments and the subsequent remarks on international monetary reform draw on my paper "Financial Interdependence and Variability in Exchange Rates," prepared for the May 1979 colloquium of the Société Universitaire Européenne de Recherches Financières (to be published by SUERF).

the monetary policy action taken in America. And because one or more key financial variables in Europe are altered, there is no way the output of goods, the price level, and the volume of employment in Europe can be completely insulated from the American action. No model of "flexible exchange rates" can yield complete insulation without resort to implausible simplifying assumptions (for example, the absence of international capital flows other than official reserve assets).

There is an element of truth in the conventional wisdom about the insulating properties of flexible exchange rates. The severity of the effects on a nation's economy of policy actions and nonpolicy disturbances originating abroad does vary according to the degree of exchange rate flexibility. And the effects of most, if not all, domestic macroeconomic policy actions taken abroad and of many types of nonpolicy disturbances are felt *less* in the home country if the national currency is permitted to appreciate in response to external stimuli that are expansionary and to depreciate in response to those that are contractional. This element of truth, however, scarcely constitutes an unqualified recommendation for more rather than less exchange rate variability. The "partial" insulation of rate variability must be seen in the light of two further, equally important points.

First, the buffering tendencies associated with variability do *not* apply to every type of disturbance originating abroad. For example, if foreign investors shift their asset preferences, reducing the proportion of home-country-currency assets in their portfolios, that disturbance will adversely affect prices and output in the home economy when its currency is permitted to depreciate in response to the asset shift; but disruptive effects on domestic prices and output can be avoided if the exchange rate can be kept the same. More generally, when financial market disturbances originate abroad, a nation's policymakers may be *least* effective in buffering the effects of the disturbance if they refrain from exchange market intervention and permit the exchange rate to float.

Second, the buffering tendencies associated with exchange rate variability are not always beneficial. Policymakers should not want their nation to be buffered against the rest of the world in periods dominated by disturbances originating within the real sector of their own economy. If a nation's policymakers take actions that turn out to have been mistakes, moreover, they will be less unhappy in retrospect if some of the consequences of their mistakes spill over into the rest of the world instead of being concentrated in their own country.

These observations imply that European policymakers should avoid an unqualified commitment to "stability" of exchange rates but instead adopt an agnostic approach to exchange rate variability. For the exchange relationships of European currencies with the dollar and other non-European currencies, there will be times when flexibility will be the right policy and other times when it will be appropriate to intervene in exchange markets to prevent flexibility. Equally important, this agnosticism should apply to exchange relationships within the EMS, at least until a much greater degree of convergence in domestic macroeconomic policies is achieved.

A third issue discussed by Triffin is the rapid growth of "offshore" Eurocurrency banking and the "overhang" of dollar-denominated assets and liabilities that has resulted from that growth.

I am unhappy with the term "overhang" used in this context. As a first approximation to an analytical description of Eurocurrency banking, I believe this growth in dollar-denominated assets should be viewed as a manifestation of growing financial intermediation across national boundaries. The Eurocurrency markets are in many respects an efficient response to the legitimate needs of private traders and investors and to the need for channeling savings in the global economy from one national financial system to another. Problems are certainly raised by Eurocurrency banking—for example, the tendency of most nations' governments to discriminate in favor of external currency banking, which leads to competitive disparities and an undesirable structure of world financial regulation. But the issues here are subtle and the remedies to the problems anything but obvious. It would be easy for governments, even though well intentioned, to do the wrong thing in trying to "control" the Eurocurrency markets.

The growth of Eurocurrency banking is part of the rapidly increasing degree of financial interdependence of the major economies. It is tempting, but nonetheless wrong, to blame Eurocurrency banking for many of the problems and tensions that go along with this increasing interdependence. We are accustomed to accepting interdependence and its implications when we consider trade and the markets for goods. We must learn to think similarly about financial interdependence and the capital account in the balance of payments.

Last, I would like to add to what Triffin says about international monetary reform, but with a somewhat different emphasis.

My point of departure is the proposition (a corollary of what I said earlier about the impossibility of insulating nations from each other) that individual nations cannot successfully pursue independent macroeconomic policies under conditions of intermediate interdependence. That proposition has fundamental implications for what it is feasible to try to accomplish by "reforming" the international monetary system.

Robert Triffin

The constraints on a nation's freedom to take independent policy actions are most apparent in its choice of external monetary policy. Two central banks in a two-nation world could not act independently to set one exchange rate at different exogenous levels; similarly, N central banks in the actual world economy cannot act independently to set N minus 1 exchange rates at N exogenous levels. Unless the world's total stock increases, one nation cannot acquire (spend) outside reserve assets without another nation's simultaneously using (receiving) them. Nor can one nation gain or lose external reserve assets in currency-denominated form without generating equivalent changes in external reserve liabilities for another country.

Because all nations cannot successfully implement external monetary policies of their own choosing, some degree of consultation and cooperation about exchange rates and external reserve positions is inevitable. This fact, a desire to foster more than minimal cooperation, and a perception of current world monetary arrangements as anarchic lead many analysts to argue that nations should agree on some new supranational rule of law for exchange rates and external reserves.

The difficulty with this rationalization for a new effort at international monetary reform is that it fails to pursue the logic of its own argument far enough. The lack of independence of national policy actions applies not only to external monetary policies but also to *domestic* macroeconomic policies.

Since nations' domestic as well as external policies are not independent, restriction of international cooperation to the area of exchange rates and external reserve positions is bound to be inadequate. From the perspective of individual nations or regional groups of nations, there is no logical dividing line between external and domestic policy decisions. Nor can the external and domestic sectors of a national or regional economy be validly analyzed in isolation. If supranational traffic regulations were written to conform to the realities of nonindependence, their scope would have to be extended to the entire range of domestic as well as external macroeconomic policies.[7]

Should national governments be urged to develop such a comprehensive rule of law for the world economy and to subject their domestic policy actions to corresponding enforcement responsibilities of supranational institutions?

7. The amended Articles of Agreement of the International Monetary Fund (in force since April 1978) mention general obligations to promote financial and economic stability (such as in Article I), but the operational emphasis (as in Article IV) is on the exchange rate policies of member countries. With the exception of a caveat and one important reference that gets the camel's nose into the tent, the Fund's guidelines for the "surveillance over Exchange Rate Policies" (adopted in May 1977) do not even mention domestic macroeconomic policies. See International Monetary Fund, *IMF Survey* (1978), p. 107.

A sufficient reason for rejecting that recommendation is its evident impracticality.

Even if domestic politics permitted national governments to yield a significant part of their sovereignty, an effort to write a comprehensive rule of law for the world economy could not deal with the most important problems caused by macroeconomic nonindependence. One must have a naive view of the role of law to accept the notion that nations can first agree on a covenant articulating rules for acceptable behavior (and proscribing certain types of behavior) and can thereafter make independent decisions without creating serious problems for each other. Laws do not (and cannot) play such an efficacious role in regulating individual behavior. Nor does a well-functioning legal system for a society obviate the need for positive collective action to supply "public goods." Cooperative decisionmaking about national macroeconomic policies is an international public good. Its supply requires discretionary collective action by national governments, not the development of sweeping laws.

For all these reasons it is not possible to devise a supranational rule of law for the regulation of macroeconomic interactions of national economies that would be both politically feasible and analytically sound. If the interdependence of national economies continues to grow as it has in the last three decades, moreover, it will be increasingly inappropriate to concentrate any "reform" efforts on the international monetary system alone.

Where does this conclusion leave international cooperation? Judged from a systemic perspective, what can be done to promote a healthy and stable evolution of the world economy? National governments in Europe and North America, as well as in the world as a whole, have three broad choices in collectively managing their economic interrelations.

One is to try to find mutually acceptable ways to "dis-integrate" the world economy, or at least to inhibit any further integration. Impediments to the movement of goods, assets, or people across national borders reduce benefits for some individuals. But they may allow more autonomy in national macroeconomic policies and, for good or ill, to a greater extent confine the consequences of policy actions and nonpolicy disturbances to the nation where they originate. If nations place a high priority on being able to experience divergent macroeconomic outcomes, efforts should be made to devise impediments that yield greater autonomy but sacrifice as few of the benefits of interdependence as possible.

A second possible course is to maintain governmental institutions and decisionmaking behavior in essentially their present form. Domestic macroeconomic policies, for example, would be made, as now, with only minimal international consultation; international monetary arrangements would permit national discretion in the choice of external monetary policy. This would be a passive posture.

The third course is to try to find mutually acceptable ways to increase cooperative decisionmaking about national macroeconomic policies and thereby improve outcomes for the world economy. This course not only would accept increasing interdependence, but would actively try to promote a corresponding evolution of national and supranational institutions to deal with it.

The passive course, I believe, is likely to be ruled out on political grounds. Controlled dis-integration, no matter how ingenious, is likely to prove either impossible or excessively costly. Difficult though it will be, therefore, I believe the best and most practical course will be to try to adapt to increasing interdependence, and thereby to manage it better. Among other things, that course implies learning the lessons of collective action internationally that have been learned (or in some cases are still being learned) by individual nations.

Whichever of the three courses one believes should characterize economic interrelations of nations in the 1980s, it should at least be clear that international cooperation should not be excessively preoccupied with the international monetary system, especially with exchange rate variability. One awkward fact is that an individual nation, or a group of nations like the European Community, is sometimes better off when exchange rates are allowed to move and at other times better off when they are not. A second awkward fact is that the behavior of exchange rates desirable for one nation or one group of nations may at times be undesirable for others. The most important economic issues faced by national governments, however, stem from the many financial and real-sector interdependencies that link them; these determine the outcome for the world economy whatever happens to exchange rates. The more policymakers and analysts allow themselves to be distracted by the artificial debate about fixed and flexible exchange rates or by narrowly conceived efforts to reform the international monetary system, the less quickly they will come to grips with the problems of interdependence.

Christopher McMahon

The Long-Run Implications
of the European Monetary System

I believe that the emergence of the EMS in 1978 was both a symptom of and
a broadly appropriate response to current economic and financial problems.
I further believe that these problems will be with us for many years to come
and that the EMS has the potential to help resolve some of them. It seems
best, therefore, to begin by outlining the way I see the underlying problems
of the international monetary system, both present and prospective and then
in the light of this analysis to indicate the implications of the EMS for global
monetary and economic developments.

My first proposition is that a regime of fully and freely floating exchange
rates is unstable, unwelcome to governments, and therefore unsustainable.
This proposition will not command universal assent. But perhaps it could be
generally agreed that, as a matter of fact, the regime of floating rates of the
past six years has not fulfilled the expectations that were widely held at its
outset. (There are differing views, of course, about whether the initial expectations were sensible or appropriate.) The volatility of exchange rates, which
was natural in the initial stages, has persisted and—for good or bad reasons—
is widely disliked by governments and business. More to the point, movements
in nominal exchange rates, which seem large and disruptive to the governments and citizens of the countries in whose currencies they occur, do not
appear to have produced the hoped-for degree of fundamental economic
adjustment.

This is partly because, as cost-price effects have been felt more quickly in
both appreciating and depreciating countries than was earlier believed or
hoped would be the case, substantial movements in nominal exchange rates
have often been reflected in small movements in real rates. But it is probably
also because real exchange rate changes have proved to be relatively weak
instruments for producing current account adjustment when set against the
dynamic and structural forces that have been at work. To take such a view

81

does not necessarily imply an "elasticity pessimism"; rather it implies a belief that in many circumstances the underlying disequilibria are such that the real exchange rate changes necessary to overcome them are so large as to be extremely difficult, if not impossible, to engineer and maintain in a normal society.

Whatever the rights and wrongs of the argument, it is a fact that the spread of surpluses and deficits has not been significantly reduced during the period of floating rates. Indeed, there is a good deal of evidence of increased polarization—the strong economies getting stronger and the weak weaker.

One response to these facts is to deny that they are relevant: to say that there is no reason to expect a particular exchange rate movement to influence a current account position—indeed, that it is misguided to look at the current account at all. A body of academic opinion holds that one must look only at the total balance of payments and that complex and subtle adjustments to this overall magnitude do indeed take place through the instruments of relative exchange rates, though fundamentally as a result of relative movements in monetary expansion. No one could deny, of course, that movements in the capital account are important and have a role to play in international adjustment, however that is interpreted. I shall have something to say about this later on. But whatever the theoretical or prescriptive value of a total balance-of-payments approach, it is stunningly inappropriate as an analysis of the stability of an actual regime of floating rates or as a forecast of how such a regime will develop.

Whether they should or not, governments show a marked tendency to pay attention to individual parts of their overall balance of payments, especially the current account and the movement of reserves. It is sometimes said that when there were no balance-of-payments statistics there were no balance-of-payments problems; and in one sense this is an illuminating remark. But the more important point is that there were tariffs before there were trade statistics.

There are many reasons why governments will always take an interest in their current account and, at least among industrialized countries, tend to have a bias in favor of a surplus. Their shoemakers and steelworkers may become impatient with the workings of an ideal monetary policy alone. More generally, an economy geared toward an export surplus tends in practice to be a high-investment, high-growth economy. A deficit, even when financed by autonomous inflows, can appear fragile; and indeed, when bad luck or bad management reduces the inflows, the resulting consequences for economic policy can be very distasteful to the government in office, especially if it is short of reserves.

Some apparent degree of control over its destiny—or at least over the movements of such a major and visible economic measure as its exchange rate—will always be a high priority for a government. Borrowing will never be as enjoyable as lending or simply watching reserves build up. An underlying stimulus to the economy from net exports is easier to live with and manage than an underlying reduction in demand from net imports. A country with a strong surplus or one with large reserves is, in practice, able to play a politically more important role in the world than its "weaker" neighbor.

Some will argue that all this is bad economics, that the power to influence the variables considered important is illusory or exists only in the short term. Nevertheless, for good reasons or bad (I happen to think many of the reasons are sensible, but that is beside the point), I suggest that it is a fact, and likely to remain so, that on balance governments prefer (1) stability of and the visible exercise of some control over their exchange rates, and (2) to be in current account surplus or building up reserves, or both.

Developments in 1978 provide powerful support for the first of these two points. The initial generating force for setting up the EMS was the wish to establish more exchange rate stability and give governments and central banks greater control over their exchange rates, at least in one part of the world. Perhaps even more striking, both the United States and Canada, probably the two countries most inclined to a market-determined exchange rate policy, showed that a point could be reached at which they were prepared both to take policy action and to intervene heavily to stabilize their exchange rates.

There is now not a single country in the world that has not been prepared to intervene strongly to prevent or moderate a movement of its exchange rate in one direction or the other. If the intervention had been concentrated in the early part of the period of floating rates, it might have been possible to argue that in time governments and central banks could be weaned from their interfering propensities and would move gradually to an orientation based exclusively on domestic policies, allowing exchange rates more and more freedom. The facts, however, suggest the reverse: that there is an underlying desire for more rather than less exchange rate stability and a willingness, which is now probably increasing rather than declining, to seek to achieve this by giving at least some priority to the management of the exchange rate itself.

Of course, to identify a general desire and determination of this kind is to say nothing about its prospects of being satisfied. Recent years have underlined the difficulties of achieving exchange rate stability. But these seem slight compared to those of achieving the second broad aim of external policy—a kind of mercantilism which, as suggested above, is widespread if not universal. It is not easy to see how everyone can be in surplus—or adding to their reserves—at the same time. However, if my analysis is along the right lines, it is easy to see why there is such economic tension and apparent lack of stability in the international economic arena at present.

The question then becomes, how can one expect ever to achieve any degree of international monetary stability? It is not accidental that the two most striking periods of such stability in modern times were achieved when one country held an overwhelmingly predominant position in the world. It was in an unchallengeably strong economic and financial position, both externally and internally; maintained near price stability; was able to practice liberal trade policies even when they were not fully reciprocated; and acted as banker to the rest of the world, both lending long term and taking deposits. The periods were, of course, the one before the First World War, when the United Kingdom was dominant; and most of the Bretton Woods era, when the United States was dominant.

In these periods, when the dominant country was strong enough to act atypically, the rest of the world *was* able to satisfy by and large its propensity for stability and mercantilism. To concentrate on the more recent period as being more relevant to present preoccupations, countries outside the United States were able to invest and grow and gradually liberalize on the back of export surpluses. All who wished to could acquire desired reserves without others having necessarily to lose them. Exchange rates were kept broadly stable but it was possible to alter individual exchange rates by government decision when the situation demanded. In this way a regime of "fixed" exchange rates probably enabled countries that were sufficiently adept to make more use of exchange rate alterations for the purpose of adjustment than they have been able to do under floating rates: other exchange rates would normally remain fixed, the alteration was signaled as a policy act, and flanking measures to help promote the volume adjustments and restrain the cost-price effects could be taken.

A third regime of fixed exchange rates based on a dominant country may be mentioned—the snake. The analogy cannot be carried too far, as Germany has refused to become a reserve center for its snake partners, and the arrangements for altering exchange rates have involved Germany in just the same way as the other members. But it has been a regime preeminently based on one dominant, high-performance noninflationary country; it has involved fixed, though sometimes adjustable, exchange rates; and it has been, despite predictions from outsiders and especially from academic economists, remarkably stable and durable. While it has not had the reserve-center mechanism for enabling members on balance to remain in surplus, the fact that it is only a part, and a highly noninflationary part, of the international monetary system as a whole has served the same purpose: for virtually every month of its existence, spanning the years of maximum OPEC surplus, the snake as a whole has been in surplus with the rest of the world. But whatever the reasons, it did not in the past prove possible for the other large EC countries—France, Italy, and Britain—to remain in the snake.

If previous periods of world monetary stability have been those in which one country has been overwhelmingly dominant, one might claim equally that instability has occurred when the reverse was true. The interwar period is legendary for the extent to which it was dominated by economic and monetary conflict and tension, reflected in poor economic performance, violent fluctuation in exchange rates, and widespread protectionism. It was also clearly a period in which the United Kingdom and sterling had lost their previous dominance and were being challenged, though they had not yet been fully replaced, by the United States and the dollar.

Perhaps even more strikingly, the past decade or so has again been a period that might be loosely described as oligopolistic. The United States, though still by far the most powerful nation and economy in the Western world, is no longer *hors concours.* Japan on the one hand and Germany on the other have become genuine rivals (to use the word nonpejoratively and with no imputation of any particular behavior). The change will be, of course, made greater by the extent to which the EC comes to be regarded as a sovereign or decision-making unit. The relative reduction in the role of the United States has been marked by the abandonment of the priority it formerly gave to its role of banker to the system. While it remains, in a certain sense, the world's banker, it has taken its place in the world of trade and payments as one of the players. This ambiguity is the source of much present and prospective tension.

This is perhaps all fairly familiar and may not appear at first sight to deserve the emphasis I am giving it in a discussion on the long-range implications of the EMS. But the reasons I believe it is important (and the point of the argument so far) are the following. First, the present oligopolistic situation is likely to persist for the foreseeable future; any changes are likely to be in the direction of some increase in the number—which will still remain small—of major powers, not in the direction of the reemergence of one superpower. Second, for the reasons I have adduced, the present and prospective situation is *inherently* difficult and, no matter how much goodwill and good economics there may be, *inherently* fraught with potential conflict and danger. Third, as is the case with any oligopoly, the present position is indeterminate: it will be

particularly difficult—much more so than is often assumed—to find any systemic solution to the obvious problems that face us.

This last point may need some elaboration. It is natural for those concerned
about the shortcomings of the present arrangements to look toward the creation of a new world system somewhat analogous to Bretton Woods but in
which the dollar would no longer be the pivot. An outside asset, the volume
and growth of which would be internationally determined, would somehow
ultimately take primacy over all domestic currencies. However, it is difficult
to see how, even in the very long term, an outside asset—the SDR—could per-
form the function of reserve base for the late twentieth century world. There
are reasons in particular for this doubt. First, while there is plenty of evidence
that countries are on balance happier increasing their reserves than reducing
them, it is the process of *earning* the increase (that is, running the surplus)
that is important in determining stable and non-beggar-my-neighbor behavior
rather than the process of simply acquiring more assets (that is, annual alloca-
tions of SDRs). The beauty of the Bretton Woods system was that, although
it was originally based on an outside asset, gold, the crucial link to gold was
only through the United States: the reserves of the system were in the first
instance provided by the United States and as a natural consequence of
developments of trade and payments between countries.

The second reason why it is bound to prove extremely difficult—to put it
no higher—to create a truly SDR-based system is that such a system, if the
SDR is to be more than a numéraire or a useful supplement to existing reserve
assets (where there is a considerable tension-reducing role for it to play), must
depend on genuine asset settlement. That is, all countries must be willing and,
through ownership of sufficient SDRs, able to settle deficits with SDRs rather
than with their own currencies. I cannot visualize how the world's major
powers are going to be put, or allow themselves to be put, in this position.
Nor do I believe it appropriate for them to be in this position, because I
believe that they could provide reasonable assurance of being able always to
meet their asset-settlement obligations—and at the same time ensure that
developments in world liquidity depended primarily on SDRs rather than on
changes in holdings of their domestic currencies—only by extremely and
inappropriately tight restrictions on the flow of long- and short-term capital
from the major banking centers to the rest of the world.

What I have been trying to suggest about the relevance of all this to the
EMS and to its long-term implications is that the development of the EMS in
its two major manifestations—an attempt to secure greater exchange rate

stability and a hope of someday establishing a new reserve asset—is natural in present circumstances. It is working with the grain of underlying economic and financial developments rather than against it. This is not to say that the EC countries are bound to succeed in their EMS aims or that, if they do succeed, there is no risk to the world as a whole from the thrust of their policies. The world is full of economic and financial danger; and it is perfectly conceivable that, wrongly handled, the EMS could exacerbate antagonism, increase instability, and lead to lower welfare generally. My point is rather that there is not a true alternative world waiting to be born, whose emergence will be frustrated by the EMS. There is not a potentially stable and sustainable world of free floating between all currencies. There is not—at least not as far as one can see—the potential for a full SDR system toward which all countries would have equal obligations. We are condemned to a multipolar, multicurrency world, to some extent a world of regional blocs. The task will be—and the test of success or failure for the EMS in the long run will be—how to render such a world as benign, stable, liberal, and interconnected as possible.

What are the long-term prospects that the EMS will, first, increase the degree of exchange rate stability between members and second, increase it worldwide? In looking at intra-Community exchange rates, it is important to stress what the objective really is. The EMS is far from being a rerun of the Werner plan of a decade ago, which aimed, by progressively locking exchange rates, to reach full economic and monetary union by 1980. This was soon recognized as being too optimistic, and by the mid-1970s the pendulum had swung back toward an emphasis on exchange rate flexibility between countries whose economies and performance diverged so widely. The EMS can perhaps fancifully be regarded as a form of Hegelian synthesis of these earlier views on the exchange rate. It is certainly envisaged that there will have to be realignments of rates from time to time, as there have been in the snake, so that in five or ten years the pattern of exchange rates in Europe is likely to be considerably different from what it is today. The goals, however, are to establish more exchange rate *order;* to prevent temporary and speculative pressure from having undue influence; and most important, to use the exchange rate to some degree as a policy lever. It is hoped that the exchange rate, together with appropriate domestic measures, can be used to improve individual country performance and nudge individual economies toward a greater degree of convergence, and in this way moderate inflation where it is high and stimulate output and demand where they are sluggish.

In my view, the political will to give more priority to the stability of exchange rates, together with the substantial and increasing degree of intra-Community trade, will probably mean that in the years ahead a substantial degree of exchange rate stability will actually be achieved. There will, of course, be setbacks and periods of individual fluctuation, and the precise exchange rate intervention mechanism may well be modified over time. The United Kingdom did not join this intervention mechanism at the outset, and it is an open question whether it will do so. But more important than the precise mechanism are the degree of commitment to exchange rate stability—which is at present high among all member states, including the United Kingdom—and the obstacles that reality places in the way of achieving it.

The differing rates of inflation are usually mentioned as the greatest difficulty. But I think this problem can be exaggerated. Quite a wide divergence of inflation rates existed among members of the snake almost from its start, but they have managed to cope with this by reasonably frequent realignments. All the countries concerned would testify to the help that membership in the snake has been in reducing their average rate of inflation.

More difficult for the working of the intervention system may be the practical problems of agreeing on how the responsibility for any necessary policy action is to be shared between members when more than one large country is involved. This is the same sort of oligopoly problem as was noted for the world as a whole. The inability of France, Italy, and Britain to remain in the snake is a warning here. But again one should remember that things are rather different this time around. The political commitment to make the EMS a success is strong, and the determination to make it so is based on a much more realistic understanding of the difficulties and the need for compromises than in the earlier attempts to lock exchange rates.

The most difficult problem, and the one about which, I believe, much more thinking needs to be done, concerns policy toward the dollar. The importance for the dollar of stability between third countries is well illustrated by recent developments in the deutsche mark and the Swiss franc. The fact that Germany and Switzerland have for a long time been remarkably "harmonized," with very low inflation rates, similar growth rates, and a good deal of bilateral trade, has not prevented movements of as much as 30 percent between the deutsche mark and the Swiss franc over the past couple of years. These have been largely due to the extent to which the two currencies have been at various times differently regarded by the markets as refuges from a weakening dollar, and to differing policies followed from time to time to prevent inflows.

Within the EC the deutsche mark has tended to be the currency most closely linked to the dollar, so that when the dollar has been weak, as in the autumn of 1978, the snake has been subjected to tension by the strength of the deutsche mark; on the other hand, when the dollar is strong, as at present, the deutsche mark is at the bottom of the parity grid.

This indicates that intra-EC stability and world stability are likely to be strongly linked. The idea that the EMS might be a boat in which participants could float happily however strong the dollar tide, though popular, is misleading. On the contrary, to achieve their own limited aims, the members of the EMS will have to score some success on the wider front. This does not mean, of course, that it will be necessary, or even possible, to fix a precise dollar-EMS exchange rate. Even the idea of broad target zones, which has some attractions, is probably premature. And of course in this field it is impossible for any or all of the members of the EMS to do anything without the acquiescence of the United States. There is a long way to go and the road is likely to be marked for some time by particular moments, such as November 1, 1978, when agreement may be reached on both sides of the Atlantic that a movement has gone too far. Even well down the road it is doubtful that precise public commitments will be possible. But closer, more continuous relationships are, I think, likely—in fact, necessary. And the EMS may help develop such relationships, as member countries whose currencies are especially vulnerable to dollar movements and those whose currencies are less vulnerable get together and try to map out the broad lines of a policy approach to the dollar.

This leads to the second major aspect of the development of the EMS in the long term: the possibility that the ECU will become a genuine reserve asset. At this stage all that is envisaged is that, through reserve pooling and credit and settlement mechanisms, the ECU will become an ultimate asset for EMS members among themselves. It is an open question whether at a later stage it may be possible for monetary authorities outside the EC—or even for the private markets—to hold ECUs. If the later stage is ever reached, this will, of course, be a development of the first importance. But even short of this, the development of the EMS itself, the setting up of the European Monetary Fund, and the use of the ECU as a full-fledged asset within the Community are bound to have a bearing on the question of the reserve base of the international monetary system.

Whether or not progress is made toward establishing the SDR as the primary asset—but particularly if it is not—the question of sharing the reserve burden of the system with the United States is clearly on the agenda for the next five to ten years. U.S. authorities have expressed willingness to consider any orderly and constructive ways of sharing the burden, and behavioral developments of recent years have already produced a situation where the deutsche mark and the yen can in some ways be described as secondary reserve currencies. It may prove necessary and appropriate in the interests of long-term stability to move further in this direction.

The matter, however, is one of great difficulty and complexity. Simply encouraging currency holders to reduce the dollar proportion of their portfolios and increase the proportions held in other currencies would be a recipe for instability. The development of any other reserve currencies will have to be broadly similar to the way in which sterling and the dollar developed: on the back of a steady structural current account surplus an even larger flow of long-term capital was established, with the counterpart appearing as deposits held with the reserve center. A prime need in the years ahead is for greater long-term capital outflows from the countries in structural surplus. This itself will help produce more exchange rate stability, but there is a chicken-and-egg problem. When Britain and the United States were building up their long-term capital outflows, exchange rates were stable, there were few competing sources of capital, and relatively low interest rates persuaded others to borrow in large volume. Now, however, the possibility of large exchange rate movements and the possibility of borrowing in dollars have so far hindered the ability of relatively low interest rates in the surplus countries to play a full part in overall adjustment. Happily, there are signs of improvement, but there is much to be done. It is hoped that the mixture of experience and attitudes within the EMS may help develop stabilizing capital outflows from the area in the years to come.

In any case, if the ECU did ultimately become a reserve asset that could be held by non-European official and private holders, no matter how organized the development was there would need to be continuous understandings and arrangements with the United States, and doubtless with Japan. Greater coordination of policies, particularly monetary policies, would be necessary, as well as dialogue and agreement with third countries to limit sudden, massive shifts in reserve preference.

In all this, there would be a major role for the IMF. Relations with the IMF constitute a third long-term implication of the EMS. The IMF has for some time faced the potential danger that it could become an institution for lending only to small and developing countries. In the past there was also a related difficulty: the Fund found it hard to exert much influence over the policies of any countries other than those that were in deficit and currently borrowing from it. A major attempt has been made to meet this second difficulty in the "even-handed" provisions for surveillance in Article IV of the revised Articles of Agreement, but it is too early to say how successful this will be.

Clearly the authority of the IMF could be challenged by the development of the EMS in both these areas. The EC countries might tend to go first—perhaps only—to the European Monetary Fund for any conditional balance-of-payments financing they needed; and the exchange rate surveillance involved in the EMS intervention regime might render nugatory, for member countries, that of the IMF. The earlier discussion indicates that I also rate highly the possibility that the ECU might become in some sense a rival of the SDR.

There is no point in dodging these issues. But when examined, they are perhaps not as disturbing as they appear at first. Most EC member countries have either not borrowed at all or borrowed very infrequently from the IMF; and if they can give each other some balance-of-payments support in the future, there will be more funds available in the IMF for the rest of the world. In any case, as the new Article IV emphasizes, in the future the Fund will have to expand its role beyond that of provider of medium-term credit. The extent to which it will be able to influence the policies of nonborrowing countries is still an open question. But there is no reason to think that the EMS arrangements will be the major stumbling block.

As far as the SDR is concerned, one's view depends, of course, on what one believes can be legitimately expected from it over the next five or ten years. A cautious view, such as my own, sees it as still likely to be playing at least a supplementary, stabilizing role; and there perhaps need be no more difficulty in its relationship with two or three reserve currencies than there has been and will be in its relationship with the dollar.

The major point is that the IMF's role and authority should not have to depend on the emergence of a formal, systemic resolution of current problems. If we are going to have to live in a world where, instead of formal general rules to be obeyed to the letter by large and small alike, there will instead be continual dialogues and shifting ad hoc agreements, a world preeminently of international monetary arrangements rather than an international monetary system—and I believe we are—the role of the IMF will indeed be important in ensuring that the bilateral discussions between EMS members and the United States, Japan, and perhaps other major countries take full account of the interests of the rest of the world. For those of us in the EMS a primary task will be to ensure that we do all we can to assist the IMF and the other multilateral institutional guardians of the liberal order, such as the General Agreement on Tariffs and Trade, to promote the ideals that have guided them for the past thirty-odd years in the much more difficult time that lies ahead.

Perhaps it all comes down to the rather trite conclusion that in the long run the EMS is likely to be helpful if it is outward-looking and harmful if it is inward-looking. But the important point is that if we are afraid it will be inward-looking we must simply work to change its approach. It will be no use hoping or expecting that it will collapse and that we can remodel the world along different lines. If the EMS did not exist, it—or something similar—would have to be invented.

Comments by William J. Fellner

I find myself in agreement with most of Christopher McMahon's propositions. There is certainly nothing in his remarks with which I would dissent in a fundamental way. But I would place my emphasis differently on a few matters.

Most important, I believe that one of the necessary conditions for the success of the EMS venture is that rates of inflation among the EMS members should converge—and converge at the lowest level existing within the group. I suppose that most of the people present would agree in principle with this proposition. Yet, I think, most would have reservations about how optimistic we should be on that score.

Inflation is a method by which contradictory policy objectives are made to appear reconcilable or compatible. When governments choose to pursue conflicting aims, inflation provides an apparent way out. The appearance is achieved because the aggregate income is enlarged in nominal terms, and the public overestimates the real equivalent of its money income. But such a policy will not achieve its objective for more than a very limited period, and the aftereffects always prove onerous.

A policy aimed at practical price stability is feasible. The United States enjoyed price stability from the early fifties until the mid-sixties. Policy actions were the cause of the inflation that followed that period, not the exploitation of market power on the part of the public. More recently, we have seen that even after a substantial inflationary interlude it is possible to restore practical stability. Germany, Switzerland, and Japan are examples.

So stable prices are feasible, once it is demonstrated that the authorities will keep nominal demand at a noninflationary level (or are moving constantly toward that level). It is not just that the Phillips curve has proved to be a very misleading tool—and one should apologize to Phillips's memory, for he did not intend it to be used to justify inflation. Other arguments that are advanced to justify this or that inflationary policy are equally misleading. In every case, resort to inflation is a matter of political expedience, at the expense of real economic progress not only in the long run but in the medium term as well.

Moreover, a promise to stabilize price trends at rates of price increase of 4, 5, or 6 percent is not credible. Few will believe that a government that promises to accommodate an "underlying" inflation rate of 5 percent will resist accommodating a rise to 6 or 7 percent if cost trends should steepen. Expectations will be established that will frustrate the promise.

I would have liked to see greater emphasis on the imperative requirement for progress toward price stability in Europe if the EMS is to endure. One of the highly impressive achievements of the postwar period has been the change in attitudes in the Western European countries, from rivalry and outright enmity to understanding of one another's problems. That achievement ought not to be risked by promising too much for the EMS. The EMS ought to be candidly presented as an experiment. It is possible to say that the member nations intend to work for greater exchange rate stability and for closer cooperation in monetary and fiscal policies without claiming that the objectives will infallibly be achieved by a specific technique. To recognize that the EMS itself has a good chance of succeeding only if its members reach practical price stability within a reasonable period would be an appropriate and helpful caveat.

One of the critical statements made in the course of this meeting is that the EMS is essentially like Bretton Woods and subject to the same limitations. In answer it was noted, quite correctly, that there are differences and that some of the lessons of Bretton Woods presumably have been learned. But Bretton Woods collapsed with a loud bang—which was predicted by Robert Triffin at a remarkably early stage—and it may not be enough to find only *some* differences in the EMS design. The real question is whether the differences are sufficient to avoid a similar end.

One favorable mark for the EMS, of course, is its regional character. The nations involved have had three decades, more or less, of cooperative endeavors. There is, as I have said, an attitude of understanding for one another's problems and that is surely a plus.

But the plus has as a corollary a significant minus. The dollar is not in the EMS. In other words, a currency of the first order of importance, outside the EMS, must be expected to behave approximately as well as the EMS currencies themselves in terms of stability. The development of serious divergences between the dollar and any of the EMS currencies—in practice, between the dollar and the D-mark—would create acute tension within the EMS.

Some of the optimism about the EMS is based on the belief that adjustments in parities will be made whenever necessary, by administrative decision, without the delays that characterized the Bretton Woods system. I am doubtful. It does not seem to me probable that frequent parity changes can be handled by administrative methods. In the first place, nobody will know by how much exchange rates need to be adjusted. Second, there is no particular reason to assume that markets will not get ahead of the authorities. Once speculative movements start, parity adjustments may be forced whether or not some basic change in economic relationships has occurred. (I agree with Henri Baquiast that there is a distinction between speculative and other capital movements, but I am afraid that it is a psychological and not an operational distinction.)

Let me explain why I believe that different rates of inflation within the EMS will not be compatible with the goal of a zone of monetary stability. I recognize that, as McMahon has pointed out, it is possible to describe a system that will operate smoothly without exchange rate adjustments in spite of different rates of inflation. As he told us, it is also true that identical rates of inflation have not always been a sufficient condition for exchange rate stability. But the longer run outlook for a workable EMS with significant inflation differences would remain dim.

We need to remember, of course, that exchange rates are not determined by price relationships alone. Purchasing power parity does not fully explain why an exchange rate is what it is. Other factors influence the actual level. But if you have differing rates of inflation over any extended period, these other factors will have to carry a continuously increasing burden if exchange rates are to be kept stable. As price relationships diverge more and more from year to year, the offsets will need to become stronger if exchange rate adjustments are to be avoided. I do not believe that this can be a sustainable process.

In principle, different trends in productivity could be a factor offsetting consistent inflation differentials, because differentials in productivity trends cumulate over time, as do inflation differentials. If steeper rates of productivity growth were to be concentrated in export industries and import-competing sectors, that might counterbalance higher relative rates of inflation in the countries so blessed. But one would hardly place his hopes for EMS exchange rate stability on a possible advantage in productivity trends in the more inflation-prone countries. The contrary seems to me more likely.

Again, capital movements can offset the pressure on exchange rates resulting from different rates of inflation. In fact, some countries may be said to be natural capital importers or natural capital exporters. For some time, a capital-importing country may be able to hold its exchange rate in the face of a price level that is rising faster than those of its partners. But it is unreasonable to suppose that the capital exporters will continue to finance ever-rising requirements for external capital as the discrepancy between price levels widens. This will hardly be the case unless the inflationary countries provide much more political safety for investors than the others, which in the present context would be an unrealistic assumption.

I come back to the real world problem: unless practical price stability can be restored, the goal of EMS exchange rate stability will not be achieved. If a period of floating rates is required to work inflation rates downward to satisfactorily low levels, then, clearly, floating will have been the right policy. Indeed, neither the Swiss nor the Germans nor the Japanese could have restored stable price levels without floating. The central objective, I emphasize, is to return to an essentially noninflationary situation in which markets and market incentives will be able to work on behalf of sustainable rates of real economic progress.

Finally, I will mention briefly the so-called overshooting phenomenon— that is, exchange rate movements that vary widely from what would be expected in the light of existing inflation rates. For one thing, it is fairly obvious that some overshooting must be expected in a dynamic situation. Apart from that, I am persuaded that some part of what appears to be overshooting is a tendency for spot rates to incorporate long-run expectations about relative rates of inflation.

Suppose, for the sake of simplicity, that people concerned with foreign exchange transactions believe that as a result of a change in the inflation outlook the D-mark will appreciate 40 percent over the coming five years. That is, the D-mark is expected to rise in terms of some other currency—say, the dollar—at an approximate 7 percent annual rate. If this is not to be reflected directly in the D-mark's spot rate, interest rate differentials will have to widen accordingly. But interest rates are strongly influenced by a large group of people who do not act on expectations about rising foreign exchange rates because they have no commitments in foreign exchange, and for them the acquisition of foreign currencies would be "speculation" rather than "hedging." Most of the dollar holders who in the present circumstances do act on expectations about the effect of inflation on exchange rates belong in a different group that is engaged in international business transactions and whose commitments lead it to "hedge" when it expects foreign currencies to rise. In consequence of the weight of the first of these two groups, interest differentials may typically be much smaller than would be the case if exchange rate expectations were fully reflected. So, as a result of interest arbitrage, the spot rate for the D-mark, in the example, will tend to jump promptly, rather than making a smooth ascent over five years at the 7 percent yearly rate. Subsequently, it will rise at a lesser rate, corresponding to the interest differential. I believe that a good share of the overshooting reflects this phenomenon.

I do not wish to conclude on a pessimistic note. It seems to me indisputable that one of the EMS objectives—exchange rate stability—depends crucially on success in bringing inflation down to a common low level. Even if it should not prove possible to accomplish this in the near future, there are means to cope with the exchange rate problem by keeping each other informed and avoiding actions at cross-purposes. The tragedy would be if the remarkable progress toward cooperation were to be checked or reversed because the European states insisted on a particular technique for achieving a specific objective in exchange rate policy.